Royal Jel

The new guide to nature's richest health food

──────Royal Jelly──────
The new guide to nature's richest health food

Irene Stein

THORSONS PUBLISHING GROUP

First published 1989

© Irene Stein 1989

British Library Cataloguing in Publication Data

Stein, Irene
Royal jelly - the new guide to nature's richest health food.
1. Man. Health. Improvement. Use of royal jelly
I. Title
613.2′ 6

ISBN 0-7225-2159-6

Published by Thorsons Publishers Limited, Wellingborough, Northamptonshire NN8 2RQ, England

Typeset by Burns & Smith, Derby
Printed in Great Britain by Mackays of Chatham, Kent.

1 3 5 7 9 10 8 6 4 2

Contents

——Acknowledgements——

My thanks go to the many people who have helped me in writing this book: to Susan Merriman and Judy Quin, who helped to give my words their full meaning; to Ann and her team for their work on the book; to Keith and Gerry, trusted friends, for all their support; to Bob Ledger for his sensitive drawings; to Stephen Hampshire for his photographic work; to the Chinese, for providing the best royal jelly in the world; and to everyone at Regina.

I am, of course, particularly grateful to royal jelly itself, for providing the energy I needed to achieve all I have achieved. Especial thanks go to my family: to Jane and Lisa for allowing me space to do everything I've done; to Jack and Sophie for providing me with the opportunity to be determined and to stick by what I believe in; and to Sophie in particular for being a shining example of the benefits of royal jelly after taking it for 15 years.

Then I should like to thank the team currently doing research into the medical evidence for royal jelly's powers. Finally, I should like to thank Brad Brown for enabling the team to grow in harmony.

Foreword

With few exceptions most useful discoveries are dependent upon a pioneer, or innovator, who stands in the face of suspicions and oppositions in order to make clear the benefits of a discovery or new product. Without such 'pioneers' we would still be earth-bound and pulling carts and wagons with animals. We'd very likely be taking drinking water from the polluted Thames river, and filling our bodies with sugar, saturated fats, red meat and carcinogens, thinking it is healthy for us because it tastes good.

Irene Stein is one of those pioneers in the western world. Her discovery of royal jelly, the benefits of which have been well known in the east for centuries, especially China, has placed her in the unique position of being an advocate for a product which is new to our way of thinking. It assaults our preconceived western judge-ments to think that anything can be quite this good. I recall my own introduction to royal jelly by Irene. When I complained of symptoms of chronic fatigue, she said royal jelly could help. With tongue in cheek I humoured her and took the fresh royal jelly she provided. Within a few weeks I was feeling more healthy and vibrant. Other symptoms cleared up as well. Still, I was reluctant to credit the product she recommended. But Irene is a pioneer and with 'true grit' she has persevered with people like myself to make the value of royal jelly known to a broad population. Today she is a leading authority on this product.

People who make a difference in the world are often motivated by a vision of service to mankind: this is certainly true of the author of this book. Irene has been committed to her own health and well-being for much of her adult life. She has been willing to push out the parameters of her own thinking about health to include the wisdom and knowledge of other cultures and to use this knowledge to nurture her own healthy body and pass it on to others. She practises what she preaches, and the advantages, particularly of using royal jelly, appear to be significant. In this way she is able, with personal authority, to support others to receive salutary benefits as well. Because she has persisted for several years to advocate royal jelly as an important product for healing many health problems, her mail is filled with thousands of appreciative comments and testimonials from people she set out to serve with her insights and knowledge of this natural product.

It is very difficult to say what impact royal jelly has had on Irene's attitude or motivation. However, those who know her, as I do, recognize her to be a woman of unique and consistent sensitivity to people. She has an unswerving commitment to lead her company to become a healthy organization which is dedicated to the well-being of its employees, while offering the public a product of significant and lasting value.

Today Irene is not alone. She has a large staff and a group of supporters who are seriously studying the reasons why royal jelly is such a rich addition to western health aids, and who are considering the further implications of its use in the future. She is no longer the lone pioneer I met several years ago trying to get a few of us to try it out, but a leading spokesperson and for a growing and more educated public. We can guess with some degree of assurance that within a few years we will see another book from her about royal jelly that will further enhance our knowledge about this amazing product that comes from the world of nature and enters our world to improve our health and well-being.

K. Bradford Brown Ph.D.

Introduction

When, three years ago, I put down my pen after finishing the last sentence of the last chapter of *Royal Jelly: A guide to nature's richest health food* (published by Thorsons), I realized that I had touched only the tip of the iceberg. Even as the book went to press, I learned about new research and novel applications for this wonderful substance. Over the months I have been delving even deeper into the subject, collating all the information I uncovered: now I feel the time is ripe for a new volume.

The truth is that I am continually intrigued and amazed by new facts which come to light about this product of the hive. There seems to be no limit to the range of products in which royal jelly can be used, no end to the beneficial effects which can be derived from this miraculous substance. Yet one mystery remains. Scientists have accounted for 96 per cent of the ingredients of royal jelly but, despite intensive research, the nature of that last 4 per cent remains tantalizingly elusive.

It is now some 15 years since I first started my own royal jelly regime of one 150 mg capsule per day, taken first thing in the morning with a glass of water. At that time I was plagued by ill health and was living on diuretics, which were sapping my energy far more than the excess water. One of the first benefits I discovered of taking royal jelly was its natural diuretic action — I could soon throw those pills away! The effect on my general level of well-being, stamina and youthfulness has continued to be felt over the years. Niggling ailments which seemed to lurk round every corner miraculously disappeared. I took a major gynaecological operation in my stride with the minimum interruption of my busy business schedule. Also, I have achieved and maintained a level of energy and a workrate which would be remarkable even in a 20-year-old, and my 50th birthday looms large on the horizon! In fact, although my business and workload have grown steadily over the years, the cumulative benefits of taking royal jelly have more than kept pace.

Of course, once I realized to what extent royal jelly was

improving my quality of life I spread the word to all and sundry, especially my own family. My mother, Sophie, is an inspiration to me and to everyone who knows her. Although she is now looking forward to her eighties, she is as bright and energetic as a woman half her age. When I first introduced her to my discovery, she was a long-time arthritic. After taking royal jelly for only a short time, her crippling pain began to diminish until, at length, it disappeared completely. Thankfully, the condition has not reared its ugly head since.

Even my two daughters thrive on royal jelly. Lisa, in particular, was very susceptible in her early years to any infectious disease which was going the rounds, from the common cold to the usual litany of childhood illnesses, and when she caught them she really suffered. This was where one of royal jelly's key benefits came up trumps. Her general health and resistance to infection received a major boost and she changed from being a frequent absentee to having an excellent record of attendance at school. As an added bonus, the royal jelly cleared up her eczema. In Lisa's teenage years, the royal jelly regime helped her to sail through her 'A' level exams and is today proving to be a valuable aid in her degree studies.

My daughter Jane derived similar benefits from taking royal jelly during her childhood. Her days of having one cold after another are now long gone. There was one thing Jane *did* catch while she was still a child, however, and that was my enthusiasm for royal jelly! Now she is a vivacious, lovely young woman, working alongside me to spread the royal jelly story, to the beauty salon world in particular.

There are many benefits to be derived from using a natural substance, as the herbalists among you will know. Indeed, the West as a whole is slowly but surely moving towards a natural approach to health improvement and maintenance. To my mind, where royal jelly is concerned, three of the principal benefits of taking it are that, in contrast to what one might call 'synthetic' remedies, there is not the slightest risk of addiction, it is non-allergenic, and the body never becomes immune to its effects.

I heartily wish that the same could be said for modern medicines. When I read about the traumas experienced by those who suffer from tranquillizer addiction, about patients having to be given increasingly large doses of analgesics as their bodies become resistant to the pain-killing effects of the medications — and, come to that, when I read about youngsters experimenting with illegal drugs in an attempt to put some sparkle into their lives, it is then above all that I really appreciate the value of what Mother Nature has provided for a mental and physical 'lift'.

It has been estimated that up to a third of hospital patients are admitted suffering from the effects of modern medicine. I am not by any means condemning conventional treatments out of hand, but I do feel that prevention of disease is so much better than any cure, and that more emphasis should be placed on the holistic approach to medicine — seeing the person as a whole, rather than treating isolated symptoms.

That being said, taking royal jelly is only part of my recipe for a healthy and happy life. Naturally, I do not smoke, although I have great sympathy for those who are having problems in kicking the habit. However, I do have the occasional alcoholic drink, but I *do* mean 'occasional'! I know my body's reactions very well and I am sensitive to its adverse reaction to even a so-called 'normal' intake of alcohol.

I am a great believer in fresh air and exercise. These days the only time many people have a breath of fresh air or exercise is when they walk the few yards from their house to their car in the morning, from the car park to the office, and the same again when they go home in the evening. Fresh air is so invigorating! I go for a brisk three- or four-mile walk every morning for the exercise, to clear out my lungs, and to clear my mind and thought processes. It works absolute wonders! On the same subject, I am a fervent believer in the benefits of doing yoga breathing exercises, thereby making the best of each breath of air while at the same time relieving tension and improving muscle tone.

When it comes to skin care products, everything I put on my face contains royal jelly, and that includes tonic and moisturizer, as well as royal jelly & vitamin E cream for any blemishes. My skin is therefore in good condition, and I wear lipstick and eye make-up to feel my best. This royal jelly skin care range has only recently come onto the market, but already it is proving extremely popular. I must say that I also owe the good condition of my hair to royal jelly. But, for an even more impressive example of hair which not only retains its look and strength but also its colour, I must again cite the example of Sophie, my mother.

Yes, it is astonishing to think that royal jelly has such remarkable effects, and in the following pages you will find many accounts of even more remarkable improvements in health and general well-being not only in people, but also in animals. Also included in my book are many amazing facts which have come to light during my research into the scientific work which has been done on royal jelly in recent years.

Even after all this time, I am still occasionally surprised at the wide range of its applications. Only a few weeks ago, I was on holiday in Israel when I cut my foot on a piece of coral while swimming in the sea. The wound was deep and bled profusely — I even wondered whether I should not have it stitched up. It was so painful that I could not even stand but, before resorting to calling in a doctor, I decided to try some natural remedies. I applied aloe vera juice, with no effect, so, that night, I cut open a fresh royal jelly capsule and applied the contents to the wound. I repeated the application on the two following nights and, to my delight and relief, the cut healed up like magic.

I am not alone in my enthusiasm for this wonderful product of the hive: the number of people who have made this marvellous substance part of their lives is growing all the time. If you are not yet a member of the worldwide royal jelly fraternity, I hope that by the time you have finished reading my book you will be.

Some people wonder whether the effect it has on them may be psychological rather than physical. I am not one of them. Far from it, because I have seen too much evidence to the contrary. For example, impressive results have been achieved by giving animals royal jelly and in such cases any 'placebo' effect can be discounted.

The fact is that, however sceptical you may be, it is impossible to ignore the *physical* changes in people who take royal jelly. One of my correspondents had been suffering from septicaemia and began to take royal jelly capsules. When she attended for her three-monthly check-up, her doctor simply said, 'I don't care what you are taking, just keep taking it. Your blood is so much improved it is now better than mine!' Need I say more?

April 1989

CHAPTER 1

_ How doth the little busy _ bee...

Bees have fascinated man since time immemorial; indeed more has been written about bees than about any other animal — except man. Literature is littered with references to bees, from Virgil, who wrote of them in his *Georgics*, to Shakespeare's 'Where the bee sucks, there suck I' and Tennyson's 'murmuring of innumerable bees' not forgetting, of course, Isaac Watts' poem entitled, 'Against Idleness and Mischief' (later to be parodied wickedly by Lewis Carroll):

How doth the little busy bee
Improve each shining hour,
And gather honey all the day
From every opening flower!

The English language, too, has numerous allusions to bees; 'busy as a bee'; having a 'bee in your bonnet'; 'a hive of industry'. . . and there are plenty more. Why? What is the reason for this long-standing fascination with the bee?

One of the most likely reasons is that, until relatively recently, the workings of a hive and the social order of the bees inside were a source of wonder and puzzlement. How do bees mate? If queens are female and drones are male bees, what sex are worker bees? What goes on inside the hive? Before I answer these questions, I should like to take you briefly through the history of beekeeping; it is a fascinating subject.

The first real record of man's exploitation of honey bees is to be found in Spanish prehistoric cave etchings, dating from approximately 7000 BC. In one of these (see Figs 1 & 1a) a man can be seen climbing up a rope to a cleft in a sheer rock face, to 'rob' the colony of its combs and carry them back down to a friend waiting at the bottom.

Moving on through history we find the first recorded instance of nomadic beekeeping: Ancient Egyptian beekeepers took their

Fig 1 Spanish cave painting

swarms with them when whole populations were moved lock, stock and barrel up or down the River Nile, depending on the season. (This practice can still be seen in parts of modern-day China, although the use of trains as transport makes the whole process much easier!)

It is interesting to note that the Egyptians were as unsure as generations of men were after them as to how bees were pro-created. They believed that bees came from the sun god Ra. Other cultures had equally odd beliefs. Africans believed that they rose out of the bodies of dead lions, while in European folklore the bee is closely linked with death and bees have to be told about a death in the family, otherwise, it is said, they will not produce honey. Given the fact that the bee was first domesticated at the end of the Neolithic period, the evolution of such beliefs is understandable. Whenever man forms close links with a species, superstitions and bizarre ideas flourish about phenomena he does not understand.

Fig 1a   Spanish cave painting detail

Although bees were originally domesticated for their honey, there is ample evidence that they were once used as weapons in several countries: 13th-century Hungary, 17th-century Germany and East Africa as late as the First World War provide examples of such original warfare. It is easy to imagine the havoc which could be wrought by hives of angry bees thrown into the middle of advancing enemy troops!

As far as beekeeping in the United Kingdom is concerned, we know that the Ancient Britons had domesticated colonies in the forests. Indeed, the British Isles were known by the Romans as the 'Honey Isles'.

It was not until the late Middle Ages that the 'skep' was developed. A skep consists of a basket made by stitching together coils of straw rope, and hives of this design are still used in parts of Europe today (see Fig 2). The Tudor House garden in Southampton for example, is a living museum of beekeeping. There the visitor can see not only straw skeps, but also bee bowls which are kept in recesses in a brick wall to protect the hives. The skep, however, was the most commonly used hive and it became quite sophisticated. Although this system bore a close similarity to the way bees live in the wild, with the entrance to the hive at the bottom and the honeycombs at the top, it did not allow for examination of the bee colony.

The modern hive used in most parts of the world is almost identical to one invented by the American clergyman L.L. Langs-

Fig 2 A skep (traditional straw)

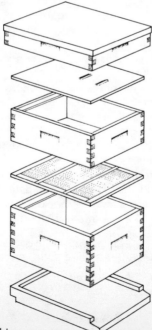

Fig 3 'Langstroth' hive

troth in 1851 (see Fig 3). This hive consists of a set of superimposed boxes inside which bees are kept on hanging comb frames. Between these frames and the box sides is a gap of between 5mm and 9mm, called the 'bee space'. Langstroth discovered that the bees would leave a 5mm gap between the box and the frame and would build the combs up to leave the same gap between them so that the bees could move around the hive. This new system made it possible to lift combs out individually on their frames so that the frames could be moved to different hives if so desired, or so that the condition of the colony could be examined.

Until the 16th century, very little was known about bees — and much of what was thought to be fact at that time turned out to be fallacy. In 1586 the world was shocked to discover that the 'sultan' or 'king' bee was in fact a queen. In the 17th century, it was first suggested that the worker bees were female and the drones male (which in essence is true, although workers only have tiny ovaries and cannot normally produce eggs). However, it was as late as 1845 that a man called Johann Dzierzon realized that drones are produced from unfertilized eggs, whereas workers and queens are produced from fertilized ones. This discovery was the key not only to good hive management but also to understanding the lives of bees.

A honeyed existence

There are three kinds of bee in a honey-bee colony: workers, drones and the queen (see Fig 4). The workers have many duties during their short life, including acting as 'nurses' to the bee larvae in their cells — feeding them and sealing them inside with wax when it is time for them to pupate — ventilating the hive, standing guard at the hive entrances to see off potential intruders and, of course, foraging for pollen and nectar to make honey. This last duty occupies the major part of their short lifespan.

As Dzierzon suggested, the drones are indeed produced from unfertilized eggs laid by the queen. Their sole task is to mate with the queen and, once they have fulfilled that function, the drones are not allowed to return to the hive but are left to die in the inhospitable outside world.

The queen is unique for many reasons, but she is unique in nature in that she can choose the sex of her offspring at will. When she mates with a drone during her mating flight, enough sperm to last her through her egglaying life is deposited in a special sac. She usually begins to lay two eggs within two or three days of returning to the hive from the mating flight. These eggs are not laid at random. When the queen finds a suitable, smallish cell for a worker bee, she inserts her abdomen into the cell and lays an egg which will have been fertilized by the excretion of a very small quantity of sperm.

Fig 4 Three bee types: queen, drone and worker

How she prevents the glandular excretion of sperm when laying a
'drone egg' is a mystery, as is much, still, about the queen bee.

So the worker bees develop from fertilized eggs laid in small cells,
while the drones evolve from unfertilized eggs laid in larger cells.
How, then, are queens produced? The egg which will develop into
a queen bee is totally indistinguishable from a 'worker egg' at the
time it is laid. The only difference is in the size and shape of the cell.
A queen cell is very much larger, stands out from the comb and
hangs down from it.

Despite the identical nature of the eggs, there are enormous
differences between the queen and the worker by the time they
reach maturity. The queen is considerably larger than the worker,
has very different inherited instincts and a remarkably different
anatomy. Her abdomen is distinctly pointed for egg-laying, she
lacks the food glands and the pollen-gathering equipment which
worker bees have, she has a larger thorax, is much longer overall,
has large, pear-shaped ovaries and a special gland from which she
excretes 'queen substance'. This substance contains a combination

of fatty acids which are related to the fatty acids found in royal jelly. In the case of the queen, however, the glandular secretions act as a pheromone — a message to all the bees in the colony that the queen is present and all is well. The queen will live for up to six years and lay more than 2,000 eggs per day.

Compare this with the much smaller worker bee whose only reproductive organs are rudimentary ovaries, who has a life expectancy of as little as six weeks and who secretes the magical substance which is the subject of this book — royal jelly.

How, then, is it possible for two eggs which are similar in all respects to develop into two such different insects as the queen and the worker bee? The answer is at once simple and extraordinary — royal jelly.

Until the eggs have hatched into larvae, which takes about three days, nothing remarkable occurs; indeed nothing remarkable occurs for several days afterwards, either. As soon as an egg hatches, be it in a worker or a queen cell, one of the worker bees will secrete a drop of royal jelly from its brood food glands into the cell. Royal jelly is continually deposited in the cell for some two to three days (it has been estimated that a larva is fed up to 1,300 times a day and that feeding during the larval stage may involve more than 2,750 bees).

It is at this point that the difference in the feeding pattern for queens and workers becomes apparent. After three days, worker bee larvae are fed a mixture of royal jelly, honey and pollen, while the future queen still receives her rich diet of royal jelly with nothing added. After eight days, both types of cells are sealed with wax while the larvae spin their cocoons, moult, and change from larvae into pupae. Within the pupae, the adult bees are forming. The worker emerges 21 days after its egg was laid, while the new queen has chewed her way out of her cell five days earlier — just 16 days after the egg was laid.

If the new queen meets any other freshly hatched queens, a fight to the death ensues. Otherwise, the virgin queen will scour the hive for any potential rivals still in the pupal stage and will kill them by stinging them through the cell walls. About a week after emerging from her cell (see colour plate section), the queen will embark on her mating flight and the cycle begins again.

Throughout her life the queen will be fed royal jelly by her worker subjects. The only time her diet varies is shortly after she emerges from her cell, when she takes a few sips of honey.

The vital factor

It is clear that the most amazing fact in this account of life within the hive is that royal jelly transforms a worker bee larva destined for a

Cinderella existence into a true queen. This has been a source of great controversy and much research for many years.

The results of this research are fascinating. To begin with, it has been proved many times (indeed, it is now accepted practice in queen-rearing) that a worker bee larva can be transferred to a queen cell before it is three days old and will still grow into a queen. The timing, though, is crucial. If the transfer is left any later, the result will be a bee which is neither queen nor worker, but somewhere between the two.

Nowadays, the scientific community is agreed that royal jelly is the vital factor in the development of a queen bee. Attempts have been made to synthesize royal jelly and to produce queens with the synthetic product in vain. Many of the larvae thus fed die at the pupal stage, and those which survive into adulthood are not full queens but queen/worker hybrids.

Superbees

Intensive research has also centred on the various strains of bee in an attempt to select the best bee for a particular purpose, whether it be for more prolific breeding, greater honey production or lack of aggression. This research has also, of course, involved cross-breeding, i.e. using drones from one strain to mate with queens from another.

There are four species of honey bee: *Apis mellifera*, the most common honey bee in the world; *Apis florea*, a tiny bee found in South-East Asia; *Apis dorsata*, also an inhabitant of South-East Asia but a very large bee which builds extremely large combs; and *Apis cerana*, also called *Apis indica*, which hails from the Indian sub-continent. The last three species are not prolific honey producers and, since man's principal purpose in domesticating bees has been to obtain honey, it is hardly surprising that *Apis mellifera* has become the dominant honey bee (see Fig 5).

Through continuous cross-breeding and mutation over the millennia, more than 20 races of bees have evolved, including the infamous Brazilian-African hybrids which acquired the reputation of being 'killer bees' when they escaped into the wild. At the other end of the aggression scale, however, is the Italian bee, *Apis ligustica*, and it is this honey bee which has attracted the most interest in recent times.

Italian bees are smaller than the original *Apis mellifera*, to which species *Apis ligustica* is closely related, but they have proved to be true superbees. Not only are they renowned for their gentleness, but they are also prolific breeders and honey producers. What is more, they have been found to be superior producers of royal jelly in regard to both quantity and quality. This is extremely fortunate

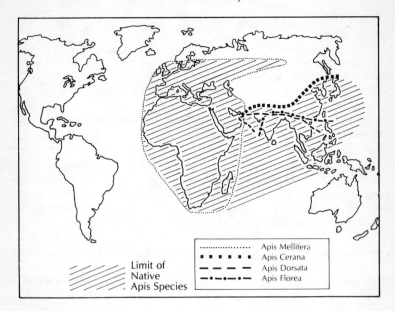

Legend:
- .... Apis Mellifera
- ▪ ▪ ▪ ▪ ▪ ▪ Apis Cerana
- — — — — Apis Dorsata
- —•—•—•— Apis Florea
- /////// Limit of Native Apis Species

Fig 5 Bee distribution

for the growing number of people around the world who appreciate the benefits of royal jelly as a dietary supplement, since the Italian bee's superiority as a honey producer means that this strain is now established in virtually every country.

As we shall be seeing later, the Chinese in particular adopted the Italian bee for breeding purposes earlier this century, and the majority of the six million domesticated bee colonies in China are now Italian. In this, as in so many other areas of apiculture, China has led the way.

Products of the hives

Of course, royal jelly is not the only bee product used by man. There are many others, of which the best known is honey. For many thousands of years, honey was the only sweetener available to man and it was only as recently as 200 years ago that its modern substitute, sugar, was processed from the sugar cane plant and made widely available. As well as honey, we shall look at three other products of the hive, pollen, propolis and, believe it or not, bee venom.

Honey

Honey is commercially available in three forms — liquid, comb and creamed. The two most frequently found are the liquid and creamed versions.

Bees manufacture honey from the nectar they collect from flowers on their foraging flights. Although, in its natural state, nectar is rather tasteless and contains up to 80 per cent water, once the worker bees have converted it into honey it is rich and sweet, with the water content reduced to about 17 per cent.

As a food, honey is hard to beat. Every part of it can be absorbed by the body and used within one hour. As such it is a source of safe, fast energy and is vastly superior to even raw sugar. Although in an ideal world we would not want our food or drinks sweetened, the truth is that few of us can claim never to crave sweet things so, if you prefer your tea or coffee sweetened, or if you find cooked fruit too tart, try using honey instead of sugar — your body will be grateful!

Apart from its delicious taste, honey also has therapeutic properties in that it soothes raw tissues; this is why a honey and lemon drink is so soothing when you have a sore throat. Honey also helps to retain calcium in the body and this is invaluable for women after the menopause when loss of calcium can lead to osteoporosis. Honey contains a significant amount of potassium, too, which helps to balance acid accumulations in the body, so it can be very useful for sufferers from arthritis and rheumatism.

Pollen

Pollen becomes a talking point every summer when hay fever sufferers keep a close eye on the pollen count to see what kind of day they are going to have; in other words, whether or not they will have to undergo the torture of continuous sneezing, streaming eyes and congestion. On this subject, it is worth noting that royal jelly can prove very helpful in alleviating the suffering of those who are allergic to pollen. A gentleman who had suffered severely with hay fever from the age of 18 began taking fresh royal jelly in October 1986. The following summer saw his symptoms much reduced and he says,

> During the current peak period for hay fever of May, June and July (summer 1988) I have had no symptoms whatsoever, even when spending eight hours walking through fields of grass and wheat at the very peak of the pollen count. This is in contrast to the fact that contact with straw, even during the winter months, for a period in excess of one or two hours would normally have been sufficient to trigger the symptoms before taking royal jelly.

It may surprise the unfortunate folk who suffer from hay fever that, in many parts of the world, pollen is used as a medicine. This is more easily understandable when you learn that it is rich in protein and amino acids and forms, with honey, the basic diet of all the bees in the hive (except, of course, for the queen). Indeed, no one has yet succeeded in 'synthesizing' pollen from other food sources with anything like as nutritious a result.

Propolis

This hive product is the least familiar to the man in the street. It is a sticky material collected by bees from buds or tree bark and used as a type of cement inside the hive, for filling in cracks and smoothing over rough surfaces. Propolis is a mixture of wax, resin, balsam, oil and a little pollen, although its precise make up depends, of course, on the plant source.

Despite the variations in the constituents of propolis, many medical uses have been found for this substance both in Asia and in the West. It seems to act both as an antibiotic and a bactericide, and as such is used in helping wounds to heal. Some practitioners have also found it invaluable in treating skin diseases, while a Russian dentist claimed that it was far superior to cocaine as an anaesthetic. For their part, many French people swear by propolis as a means of getting rid of colds and boosting the immune system.

Propolis has probably been the subject of even less research than royal jelly, but it is clear that there are very strong grounds for such work.

Recently, I was invited to visit the Apitherapy Hospital at Lianyungang in China where only bee products are used in the treatment of patients. There I learned that propolis is used to reduce cholesterol levels in the blood and that the Chinese are actively researching medical applications of all these products of the hive. Hopefully such work will also be carried out in the West soon.

Bee venom

As any beekeeper will tell you, being stung by a bee is always a painful experience, no matter how many years one has been an apiarist. However, bee venom does contain beneficial substances, including carbohydrates, lipids, free amino acids, peptides, proteins and enzymes. The peptides, in particular, have an anti-inflammatory effect, and in that same Apitherapy Hospital honey bees are induced to sting the inflamed joints of arthritic patients. At the same time, the bees are made to sting the patients on the relevant acupuncture points.

Honey, pollen, propolis and bee venom are all remarkable substances which make considerable contributions to the health of human beings. In my view, royal jelly is an even more astonishing substance, both in terms of its make-up and its effects, as the following chapters will show.

CHAPTER 2

──A recipe for success──

You might well think that, since nearly every mystery in the universe has been solved, analysing the ingredients of royal jelly would have been child's play by comparison. Unfortunately, the truth is that one insuperable problem remains: although scientists have succeeded in analysing 96 per cent of the contents of royal jelly, 4 per cent resolutely defies even the most sophisticated technology of this electronic age.

Many of royal jelly's beneficial effects can be explained by reference to its various ingredients, but others appear to have no connection with the known constituents or to be more dramatic than one might expect given the quantities involved. Whether these effects are due to that mystery 4 per cent, no one can say, and theories abound concerning the composition of that tantalizing fraction. Does it, as Professor Fang Zhu of the Lianyungang Apitherapy Hospital believes, contain an antibacterial substance which increases the number of white blood cells? Is it some substance found nowhere else in nature? Certainly, as we shall see, one ingredient in royal jelly *is* found nowhere else.

Whatever the make-up of that mysterious 4 per cent, there is yet another puzzling aspect to royal jelly and that is its synergetic effect. Synergy is a very fashionable word which is often misused, but in the case of royal jelly it is very appropriate, for the effect of the *whole* is indeed greater than that of each *part* taken individually. I asked all the professors I met in China why royal jelly is so beneficial and they replied, without exception, that the benefits could not be traced back to specific ingredients but were the result of all the different ingredients acting together. Royal jelly puts the body's systems back into balance and this is most probably due to the similar balance between the different ingredients which are present in just the right quantities to produce the maximum effect. I should stress at this point that the quantities referred to are very small indeed — there is not the slightest danger of taking an excess of any particular ingredient!

When you remember that it is a 100 per cent natural substance, used as a complete food by one of God's creatures, this all-round balance becomes a perfectly logical phenomenon. After all, if you consider that breast milk contains everything which a baby needs for at least the first six months of its life and that royal jelly contains everything which a queen bee needs for the whole of her life, then the extreme richness of this natural substance in ingredients which are essential to health, development and a balanced metabolism is easier to accept.

Does the fact that royal jelly plays such a crucial part in bee nutrition necessarily mean that it can realistically be mentioned in the same breath as breast milk and accorded a key role in our own nutrition? I believe it does and I can bring one startling piece of evidence to support my belief. In 1966, in the Department of Paediatrics at the University of Florence, 42 infants, including premature babies, were fed royal jelly with impressive results. The babies gained weight, their red corpuscle counts increased and the assimilation of protein into the bloodstream was greater than that induced by any other known treatment of malnutrition.

I should like to take the breast milk analogy a little further. If you were to analyse breast milk from 100 mothers you would find that its composition varied signficantly according to the diet of the mother. There might even be detectable quantities of drugs in the milk if the mother were on certain medication. Now, although, in an ideal world, every baby would have milk from its own mother, babies who are fed from 'milk banks' consisting of donated breast milk fare very well. Indeed, until relatively recently, the practice of wet-nursing was a common one in Western society.

Now let us look at royal jelly. Its composition does differ slightly depending on the diet of the worker bees who produce it. It will vary according to the source of nectar and pollen which the bees bring into the hive and may even contain chemical substances (rather like the drugs in certain mothers' breast milk). However, providing the raw materials for the food end product have not been treated with chemical pesticides or subjected to other environ-mental pollution, the quality of the royal jelly produced is first-class. The best fresh royal jelly on the market originates in China, where the producers are careful to ensure that the source plants are not polluted by chemicals, but I cannot vouch for the cut-price royal jelly products which have been flooding the market recently.

It may seem a cause for concern that, according to the location of the hive from which the 'bee milk' (as royal jelly is sometimes called) is collected, the composition of the substance will vary. As I have already implied, any chemical plant treatments may conta-minate the royal jelly, but also the type of plants from which nectar and pollen are scavenged can subtly alter the end product. In addition to these factors, the precise nature of royal jelly produced by a given worker bee may vary during the insect's feeding life and depends too on the time of year.

However, we have no need to worry. As long as there are no chemical contaminants and the royal jelly is preserved in its fresh state, the effects on our health will be identical, no matter what the plant source of the royal jelly we buy in the shops.

That being said, it is slightly bewildering, but understandable, to see variations in the analyses of royal jelly which have been issued by the world's laboratories. It is therefore worth looking at all these analyses when deciding which are the proven constituents of royal jelly. Certain elements are always present, whereas others may occur only rarely, according to the prevailing climatic conditions and the geographical location of the bee colony from which the substance was collected.

A good basis for discussion is the representative analysis produced in 1986 by the Cardiff County Public Health Laboratory, given below.

Water	24.00%	(weight in weight)
Carbohydrates	15.00%	(w/w)
Nitrogen	50.00%	(w/w)
(equivalent to	31.00%	(w/w) of protein)
Phosphorus	0.70%	(w/w)
Sulphur	0.40%	(w/w)
Mineral matter	2.00%	(w/w)

The mineral matter contains the following trace elements: iron, manganese, nickel, cobalt, silicon, chromium, gold, mercury, bismuth and arsenic.

The following vitamins are present:

Vitamin B1 (thiamine)	1.2 –7.40 mg/100 gm
Vitamin B2 (riboflavin)	5.2 –10.00 mg/100 gm
Vitamin B3 (niacin)	60.0 –150.00 mg/100 gm
Vitamin B5 (pantothenic acid)	65.0 –200.00 mg/100 gm
Vitamin B6 (pyridoxine)	2.2 –10.20 mg/100 gm
Vitamin B12 (cyanocobalamin)	0.15 mg/100 gm
Vitamin C (ascorbic acid)	12.0 mg/100 gm
Vitamin H (biotin)	0.9 –3.70 mg/100 gm
Inositol	80.0 –150.00 mg/100 gm
Folic acid	0.2 mg/100 gm

Before I go any further, I think that I ought to deal with two items in the above analysis which may have readers throwing their hands up in horror and their valuable royal jelly into the dustbin. Yes, royal jelly may contain traces of mercury and arsenic, but there is not the slightest need to panic. To begin with, both are present in such tiny quantities as to be hardly worth mentioning, but I would also wager that most people are unaware that we all have both mercury and arsenic in our bodies already.

Arsenic, in particular, has gained a very bad press due to its one-time popularity as a way of disposing of one's nearest but not dearest and also undesirable rodents. Although arsenic is a very powerful poison, it is only toxic when administered in the pure chemical state. When it is combined with other substances it loses its toxicity and any surplus arsenic not needed by our bodies is simply excreted. You may think that we do not actually *need* to have arsenic in our bodies, but even scientists are not sure of this — witness the fact that it has been classified as a mineral which is 'possibly essential', meaning that a *lack* of arsenic may perhaps be harmful! It is also worth noting that for many years arsenic was a common pharmaceutical ingredient and is still used in homoeopathy. Whether these metals are essential or not, our bodies need to be cleansed of any excess. This job is done very efficiently by vitamin C, which royal jelly contains, of course!

I should now like to look at what all the various 'ingredients' detected by the Cardiff laboratory can do for us. You may find this long list daunting, but I do not intend that you should read it right through at one sitting; rather, you should dip into it, using it as a reference source. Indeed, if you were to study the attributes of each ingredient in royal jelly, you would probably become convinced that you were suffering from a deficiency of every one. It's rather like studying a medical dictionary — all the symptoms seem worryingly familiar!

Carbohydrates

There was a time when the word 'carbohydrates' struck fear into the heart of weight-watchers everywhere, but today the chief enemy of slimmers has been identified as saturated fat. Indeed, carbohydrates have vital work to do in the body: they are energy-producing compounds which keep our blood sugar levels up and help the body to store protein. The carbohydrates in royal jelly are composed mainly of sugars.

Nitrogen

People rarely talk about nitrogen when discussing nutrition, but without it we would not have proteins, and we all know about the importance of proteins: they are necessary for life. Strictly speaking however, it is not the proteins which are vital to us, but rather the amino acids, which are the building blocks of protein. The other 'ingredient' in proteins is, in fact, nitrogen: the nitrogen bonds with the various amino acids to form proteins. As you can see from the Cardiff analysis, the proportion of protein in royal jelly is considerable, so the amino acids which it contains are well worth analysing and discussing.

Amino acids

The protein content of royal jelly has been analysed by many laboratories and most of the amino acids known to man have been detected, including alanine, arginine, aspartic acid, glutamic acid, glycine, histidine, isoleucine, leucine, lysine, phenylalanine, proline, serine, threonine, tyrosine and valine.

Amino acids are classified as 'essential' or 'non-essential', not according to whether we need them for our health (we need them all), but according to whether our bodies can manufacture them or not. The 'essential' amino acids are the ones which we cannot synthesize ourselves and which therefore have to be obtained from our food intake or from dietary supplements.

As with many other supplements, there would be no point in taking amino acids on their own, since our bodies need vitamins B6, B12 and niacin to be present before the amino acids can be used. If you glance at the analysis of royal jelly given above, you will see that all three are present. This underlines the importance of not looking at the ingredients of royal jelly in isolation — it is the combination of them all which makes royal jelly such a perfectly-balanced, nutritious and highly effective substance.

So, let us look at what some of these amino acids can do for us when, as in royal jelly, they are present with the various other ingredients needed for them to play their full part in keeping us healthy.

Arginine

Arginine is particularly important to men as it helps to increase their sperm count and therefore can help with sub-fertility problems. It is also vital for every adult whether male or female from the age of 30 onwards, since the pituitary gland stops secreting this substance at that time. You may think that this does not matter, but arginine is needed to synthesize and release growth hormone from the pituitary gland, and it is this hormone which helps to keep our weight stable and our figures in shape!

Aspartic acid

Royal jelly contains a relatively large proportion of this amino acid which has two functions. Firstly, it eliminates excess ammonia from the body, thereby protecting the central nervous system. Secondly (and probably more importantly since the end result is so noticeable), it is an energy booster. Research carried out in the l970s revealed that when athletes are given aspartic acid salts their stamina is noticeably increased. It would appear that aspartic acid is partly responsible for the energizing effect of royal jelly.

Glutamic acid

Glutamic acid has a somewhat similar function to aspartic acid. It too affects ammonia but, rather than eliminate it from the body, it converts ammonia into glutamine. Now this is another 'wonder substance', in that it is believed that it is able to raise IQs. This would seem enough of an achievement for a single amino acid, but it can also help with alcoholism, speed up healing, and it has a beneficial effect on depression, fatigue and sexual impotence. Glutamic acid and glycine (see below) are also believed to perform a vital role when combined in delaying ageing, building up the body's resistance to tumours, relieving allergies and helping with diabetes, hypoglycaemia and arthritis, as well as alleviating the side-effects of chemotherapy and radiation in the treatment of cancer.

Glycine

A sweet-tasting amino acid, glycine also has several strings to its bow. It boosts the pituitary gland function and muscle function, which accounts for its use in the treatment of muscular dystrophy. It is also used to treat patients with hypoglycaemia (low blood sugar) and is included in many antacid medicines.

Histidine

Although this amino acid is synthesized in the body, it is categorized as an essential one for infants and children since it cannot be manufactured in adequate quantities during periods of rapid growth.

Lysine

Lysine is one of the essential amino acids and it is especially helpful for those people who find it hard to concentrate, are losing their hair, or suffer dizzy spells, as they may be suffering from a lysine deficiency. Lysine's main functions are tissue repair, aiding growth, and producing hormones, enzymes and antibodies.

Phenylalanine

This is another of the essential amino acids and it plays a vital role in our bodies. It is a neuro-transmitter, sending signals from our nerve cells to our brains. When you increase your phenylalanine consumption, you should find any depression lifting, your memory and general mental capacity improving, your appetite for food decreasing and your appetite for sex increasing! That's quite a repertoire for one little amino acid, but this is one of those essential acids which we cannot manufacture for ourselves, so it is evidently very important that we have our daily dose, if not from our diet then by means of a royal jelly capsule.

Tyrosine

Tyrosine is not an essential amino acid, but it is closely linked with phenylalanine and, like all the amino acids, is vital to our health. Some phenylalanine is transformed into tyrosine in our bodies to perform the mood-lifting and appetite-suppressing functions. If the phenylalanine is needed elsewhere, not enough tyrosine will be provided to do these jobs, and we would be suffering from a tyrosine deficiency, with consequent depression and increased appetite: not an attractive prospect!

———————————————— Minerals ————————————————

To show the importance of minerals in our body, it is interesting to look at the major elements which make up the human body and how they combine:

Oxygen 65 per cent
Carbon 18 per cent
Hydrogen 10 per cent
Minerals 3.5 per cent
Nitrogen 3 per cent

About 90 per cent of the oxygen combines with 7 per cent of the hydrogen to make water, which accounts for an astonishing two-thirds of our body weight. Then the two minerals sulphur and phosphorus act with the rest of the hydrogen and oxygen, as well as some of the carbon and nitrogen, to make our 'organic compounds' — fats, proteins, carbohydrates, etc — which alone constitute 90 per cent of the solid parts of our body.

We constantly hear about the importance of vitamins for health, but minerals are even more important, for two reasons. To begin with, we can manufacture vitamins in our bodies, but we cannot manufacture minerals. If the minerals are not in our food, then we go without. With the advent of refined foods and the use of commercial fertilizers, the amount of minerals in our food and in much of the soil used for food production is out of balance. Even a slight alteration in the level of important minerals can have a drastic effect on our health.

So, let us look at the various minerals in royal jelly, beginning with the two main ones — phosphorus and sulphur.

Phosphorus

The bulk of the phosphorus in our bodies is in our bones, but this mighty mineral plays a very important role in other areas, too. One of its most interesting functions, given the beneficial effect of royal jelly in this respect, is in keeping the skin, hair and nails in peak condition. Improvement in all three is often one of the first benefits observed by those who take fresh royal jelly regularly. Also, phosphorus is required by the nervous system, to protect it from stress and to improve brain function. This is the reason for fish being called 'brain food' since it is particularly rich in phosphorus. Phosphorus tones up our circulation and is needed to process carbohydrates and fats.

In many of these tasks, phosphorus combines with calcium and, although the Cardiff analysis of royal jelly's constituents does not include it, many other royal jelly analyses *have* indeed identified large amounts of calcium. This discrepancy is probably due to the differences in honey-bee diets, as I mentioned earlier in this chapter.

Sulphur

Think of sulphur and you probably think of matches; indeed, it may be somewhat alarming to ponder on the fact that our bodies contain a mineral which is used in making fire! However, sulphur, like so many minerals, is invaluable to us and has a host of beneficial properties. It speeds up our metabolisms, cleans out our digestive tracts, oxidizes our blood and has a dynamic effect on many skin conditions, including psoriasis and acne. This last will ring a bell with many users of royal jelly and Vitamin E cream, since many skin conditions respond magnificently to the cream as well as to royal jelly taken internally.

Another interesting fact about sulphur is that the hormone insulin is a sulphur compound. In an American study, Kramer et al isolated peptides from royal jelly which had very similar properties to human insulin. Whether these peptides act like insulin in humans has yet to be established and could be a fruitful area for further research.

Trace minerals

The 'trace minerals' are, as the term suggests, present in only small quantities in our bodies. Do not be misled into thinking that they are unimportant, and that it does not matter if we do not get enough of them. They *are* important, and it *does* matter. If you are baking a sponge using plain flour with baking powder as a raising agent, and you leave the baking powder out, the result will be a very flat cake. The baking powder may be only a tiny part of the ingredients as far as relative quantities are concerned, but without it, the recipe will be a failure. The same applies to trace minerals: we may need only a tiny amount of them, but without that tiny amount our bodies will not function properly.

Iron Most people are aware that our bodies need iron, and that a lack of it causes anaemia. With iron-deficiency anaemia, there is not enough oxygen-carrying haemoglobin. This means that the red blood cells become pale and smaller so that they cannot distribute oxygen efficiently around the body. The result is physical tiredness, depression, forgetfulness and reduced mental functions.

The iron in royal jelly seems to do its job well, since royal jelly has been shown in several experiments to boost haemoglobin levels considerably. There is, however, another ingredient in royal jelly which plays a key part in raising haemoglobin levels, (see page 40).

Manganese Nobody has as yet identified the effects of a deficiency of manganese in humans, although poultry lacking this mineral do not grow to their full size and have bone abnormalities, reproductive problems and anaemia. It is thought that one effect of manganese deficiency may be an increased tendency towards diabetes.

Nickel Nickel is not, as far as we know, essential to our well-being. That being said, it is found in newborn babies and, since nature always seems to know best, it may well be that nickel plays a part in tissue building.

Cobalt Cobalt is naturally present in vitamin B12, contained in royal jelly. Whether all the cobalt is present in this form has not been ascertained. Cobalt is used in hospitals to treat deep-seated cancers and it may be that the cobalt in B12 acts in a similar fashion, hunting out and destroying precancerous or cancerous cells, although this is open to question. Certainly it would be logical to assume that cobalt may have that function when present in vitamin B12, and that in so acting it might offer some protection against cancer.

Silicon The value of this mineral has only recently been appreciated It is instrumental in preventing the progress of arthritic diseases and, like phosphorus, it contributes to healthy nails and hair. This clever trace mineral also keeps the protective sheaths round our nerve fibres in tip-top condition.

Chromium Chromium, like manganese, seems to have a link with diabetes. Without it, insulin cannot do its job and our bodies cannot metabolize cholesterol. The effect of chromium deficiency can be seen when we compare the results of a traditional Japanese diet with those of a modern Western one. The Japanese have five times as much chromium in their bodies as we do, and consequently suffer less from diabetes and hardened arteries. Sadly, with the introduction of our 'fast food' culture, the incidence of such life-threatening conditions is now increasing.

Gold and bismuth Neither of these minerals plays any part in human nutrition, or at least, no use has yet been identified for them! However, in small amounts they are not toxic, either. Bismuth is, in fact, used in some proprietary stomach medicines, while gold injections are occasionally used to treat arthritis.

Before I leave the topic of minerals, it is worth mentioning that nearly all the essential minerals and trace elements have been detected in royal jelly at one time or another, including calcium, potassium, copper, zinc, sodium and magnesium.

Vitamins

I am sure vitamins need hardly any introduction. Multi-vitamin supplements crowd the shelves of chemists and healthfood shops, and are becoming increasingly common sights in supermarkets. We all know about vitamin C's role in combating colds, and it is more or less common knowledge that vitamin B6 is very helpful in treating pre-menstrual tension.

Here again, we should remember that it is pointless to take many artificially-produced dietary supplements in isolation. Vitamins, like minerals, interact with other vitamins or minerals to produce a required effect, and a lack of any given vitamin may also involve a lack of others.

Come to that, it has been shown that synthetic supplements can throw the body's balance completely out of kilter, whereas natural sources of vitamins and minerals somehow do not have this deleterious effect. What we are all striving for is a perfect balance, and only by taking a well-balanced, wholly natural supplement can we hope to achieve this result. Royal jelly may not be the only natural substance to offer a recipe for success, but, rather like oil of evening primrose, it not only seems to be good for us, but also has dramatic effects on a range of ailments — without side effects! What more could one ask for?

Vitamin B1 (thiamine)

We need thiamine to convert carbohydrates into mental and physical energy. Children, in particular, need plenty of this vitamin as they are growing. If you are lacking in thiamine, you may well feel tired and depressed, have difficulty concentrating, and have little interest in food. Symptoms of a severe deficiency are swollen ankles and pins and needles in your lower limbs, though, of course both of these may be attributable to other causes.

Vitamin B2 (riboflavin)

Once upon a time, our diet was rich in vitamin B2 from unpasteurized milk, free-range eggs and other dairy produce which had not been 'tampered' with. Because of modern production methods, our riboflavin intake has been reduced dramatically, resulting in cracked lips, mouth ulcers, sore eyes and dermatitis. As with a lack of thiamine, a vitamin B2 deficiency can also result in depression and apathy. Clearly, we are doing ourselves an enormous favour if we make sure that we have enough of both these vital vitamins.

Vitamin B3 (niacin)

If you thought that the symptoms of thiamine and riboflavin deficiency were bad enough, wait until you have read what those poor people who go short of niacin could suffer (and I am talking about roughly half the population!). Indigestion, stomach pains, irritability, forgetfulness, headaches, swollen gums, insomnia, swollen tongue, loss of appetite, dermatitis, dizziness, tiredness, nausea and nervousness are some of the symptoms: it's not a very pretty picture, is it? Severe deficiency, which is admittedly rare these days produces pellagra, a particularly unpleasant disease characterized by diarrhoea, dementia and chronic dermatitis. Also if you are a smoker, you should know that the nicotine in your cigarettes releases adrenalin into your body and, if your niacin levels are low, your adrenal gland becomes very confused and starts sending equally confused messages round your nervous system!

Vitamin B5 (pantothenic acid)

Pantothenic acid is a relatively recent subject for research, and it has been found to have many startling properties. One of the most startling is that prematurely greying hair can be restored to its normal colour if the cause of the greying was a vitamin B5 deficiency! This may surprise you, but I can well believe this discovery since I have heard of several cases of grey hair reverting to its original colour after a course of royal jelly capsules.

   I have been describing what is, of course, purely a cosmetic benefit, but it does reflect the fact that royal jelly is the richest natural source of vitamin B5. White, Handler and Smith in *Principles of Biochemistry* say,

In general the distribution of pantothenic acid resembles that of the other B vitamins; yeast, liver and eggs are among the richest sources . . . royal jelly (prepared by the bee colony for the nutrition of the queen bee), and fish ovaries (before spawning) are the richest known sources of this vitamin.

What else can pantothenic acid do for us, apart from contributing to attractive locks? Its most important use is in treating arthritis, and I shall be looking at this in detail in Chapter Seven. In addition to this, vitamin B5 helps wounds to heal, fights infection, prevents fatigue and alleviates dermatitis. If you have insufficient pantothenic acid in your diet, you may well have symptoms of hypoglycaemia, blood or skin disorders, and even duodenal ulcers.

Vitamin B6 (pyridoxine)

Vitamin B6 is another very versatile aid to health. It is indispensable in the production of red blood cells and antibodies and can relieve the misery of morning sickness in pregnant women. Also, pyridoxine keeps the nervous system and the skin in peak condition, as well as helping with the digestion of fats and proteins. As I mentioned in the introduction to this section, vitamin B6 has proved helpful in the treatment of pre-menstrual tension. Anaemia and dematitis can result from a deficiency of this vitamin, so you owe it to yourself to make sure you get your daily quota!

Vitamin B12 (cyanocobalamin)

You may be thinking by now that anaemia can be a symptom of almost any vitamin deficiency, and the facts on vitamin B12 will only serve to reinforce this notion. Yes, anaemia can be caused by B12 deficiency too, in addition to general tiredness, irritability and poor brain function.

This vitamin has been used to treat a wide variety of disorders, from coeliac disease to muscular dystrophy, but it is more generally given to increase energy levels, improve the condition of the blood and the nervous system, and to stimulate growth and appetite in children.

Vitamin C (ascorbic acid)

I have some more bad news for smokers: every cigarette you smoke depletes your vitamin C reserves considerably. If you smoke 20 a day, you will need to eat 40 oranges during the day to keep your vitamin C intake up at the level required for health! Alcohol has a similarly destructive effect on vitamin C: even if you drink only occasionally, you will need to boost your intake of this valuable vitamin.

Vitamin C has a reputation for being the arch enemy of the cold virus, although this claim has still not been satisfactorily proven. What is indisputable is that vitamin C is vital for the growth and repair of body tissues: in fact, it works best as a tissue repairer and wound healer when taken with vitamin B12.

If you are not getting enough of this precious vitamin, your gums are probably spongy and bleed easily, your teeth in poor condition and your face a mass of tiny broken veins.

Vitamin H (biotin)

The symptoms of biotin deficiency will sound familiar by now: restricted growth, dermatitis and anaemia. This vitamin is destroyed by egg whites, antibiotics and alcohol, so if you have any of these three regularly, you should increase your biotin intake with royal jelly.

But is biotin that important? Yes, it is. Due to its sulphur content, biotin boosts our resistance to infections, as sulphur is the main cleansing agent in our bodies. Also, biotin is needed if fats and proteins are to be metabolized efficiently, and it helps to keep our skin clear and healthy. It is believed that vitamin H may even aid in preventing premature baldness.

Inositol

One of inositol's most important functions is to combine with choline to form lecithin which metabolizes fats and cholesterol, thus warding off coronary disease. Lecithin also has an uncanny ability to redistribute fat around the body which can be useful if you have too much fat in all the wrong places! Inositol will also make sure that your hair is healthy and glossy while at the same time helping anyone who is prone to eczema.

If you drink a lot of coffee or tea, the inositol in your body will be struggling to do its job, so you will be particularly susceptible to eczema and problems of fat intolerance.

Folic acid

Folic acid is sometimes referred to as vitamin M and must be in correct balance in a woman's body if she is to conceive and in ample supply during the months that follow. Elderly people are also known to require more folic acid than the rest of the population.

This is one of the many vitamins which are destroyed by heat and storage so, if you rarely eat freshly picked raw green vegetables, mushrooms and beans, you are probably short of folic acid. Also, if you drink more than moderate quantities of alcohol you will be destroying any folic acid in your system and could develop a severe vitamin M deficiency, running the risk of developing nutritional megaloblastic anaemia as well as digestive disorders.

Hormones

I mentioned earlier the presence of insulin-like peptides in royal jelly. An equally startling discovery has been made by scientists in recent years: some samples of royal jelly have been found to contain the male sex hormone testosterone. This would obviously be good news for men, but you will be relieved to learn that it would also be good news for women. We all, men and women, contain both female and male hormones, but in different proportions of course. In women, testosterone is produced in small quantities in the ovaries and adrenal cortex to stimulate the female libido. No, women who take royal jelly will not develop beards and hairs on their chests, but they may have an even more enjoyable love life!

The magical fatty acid

You would be forgiven for thinking by now that royal jelly almost has too many marvellous ingredients for its own good, and it *is* difficult to believe that any natural substance can have quite so many beneficial properties (and yet still be scorned by many in the scientific community). However, there is yet another miracle worker hidden away inside royal jelly, and this is a fatty acid with the imposing name of hydroxydecanoic acid.

One remarkable fact about this fatty acid is that it appears nowhere else in nature. Another is that it shows clear bactericidal properties. In tests carried out as long ago as the 1930s, hydroxydecanoic acid was found to kill the harmful organisms *Escherichia coli* and *Salmonella typhosa*. These findings were confirmed 30 years later when Blum and his colleagues discovered that penicillin was only four times as powerful on some organisms as this fatty acid, and that the acid had approximately the same power relationship with chlorotetracycline.

Another benefit of hydroxydecanoic acid proved to be a yeast-inhibiting function, which could be helpful for sufferers of such annoying and sometimes debilitating conditions as thrush and athlete's foot.

At the end of the 1950s, came an even more astonishing finding. Townsend and his co-workers demonstrated that both fresh royal jelly and pure hydroxydecanoic acid prevented the development of transplantable leukaemia, and that they could even prevent the development of abdominal tumours in mice. Part of the reason for this leukaemia inhibition may lie in the fact that royal jelly improves both the number and condition of white blood cells. In fact, hydroxydecanoic acid seems to have an all-round beneficial effect on the blood, as it has been found to increase the haemoglobin content in the red blood cells as well.

I am sure you will agree after this exhaustive analysis of the common ingredients of royal jelly that if a nutritionist were to sit down and try to devise a perfect all-round dietary supplement, he would come up with one which was not that far removed from royal jelly! However, no one has yet succeeded in producing a synthetic supplement which even comes close to the 'perfect' solution. How fortunate we are, therefore, that Mother Nature has seen fit to provide us with a ready-made recipe for success, complete with all the benefits which are unique to natural foods, such as a lack of side-effects, perfect compatibility and interaction between the many ingredients!

CHAPTER 3

—— A consumer's guide ——

Now that I have described all the good things in royal jelly and what they can do for you, you are probably wondering where you can obtain it and in which form you should take it.

As for where royal jelly is on sale, you will find the basic products, described below, in most leading chemists, health food shops and department stores. With regard to the form in which you should take your royal jelly, the first consideration, which I cannot over-emphasize, is that you should take it *fresh*, not freeze-dried. I shall be explaining the scientific basis for this recommendation in Chapter 5, but to my mind and the mind of thousands of other people there really is no comparison between the two as far as potency and effectiveness are concerned.

You could be tempted to use freeze-dried royal jelly because it is substantially cheaper, but in the realm of royal jelly you really do get what you pay for. This maxim applies even to products containing fresh royal jelly, because purity, quality and the *amount* of fresh royal jelly in the product will all affect the retail price. Another factor which is reflected in the product's price is the type of preservative used. I have always been convinced that only natural preservatives can keep fresh royal jelly in peak condition, and my conviction is still as firm as ever. Some of the less expensive brands in the shops use cheap, unsuitable preservatives which enable the price to be kept down, but at the expense of quality!

If you have never used royal jelly before, my advice is to begin with the essential ingredient of any royal jelly regime — the daily capsule.

—————— Royal jelly capsules ——————

To gain long-term benefits from royal jelly, you have to take it long term, too. This is why nearly everyone I know who swears by royal jelly uses the capsules as a basic essential of daily life, taking one capsule first thing in the morning on an empty stomach.

You will not see the effects instantly; in fact, I recommend that you take a 3-month course of capsules before you decide whether royal jelly is for you or not. Some people feel the difference after only a week or two, whereas others have to wait that much longer before they notice a change for the better. There are two reasons for this disparity. Firstly, individuals' metabolisms differ, both in the speed of reaction and in the degree to which they are out of balance and, secondly, some people are more sensitive to changes in their bodies.

Usually, the first improvement noticed is in energy levels. A Corby lady began taking the capsules with very low expectations.

I didn't honestly believe royal jelly would do anything for me. But I seem to have a burst of energy and get up and go, and well, it's lasting. I am cleaning the house from top to bottom, and am eager to get on with the garden. I am even having to curb my enthusiasm to get on with one job after another. I wouldn't have believed it!

More intransigent problems may take longer to respond, but it is worth being patient since there seems to be virtually no limit to the conditions which royal jelly can improve. I have been amazed to hear of several ladies (including a no-nonsense business executive) who are convinced that their grey hair is reverting to its original colour because they have taken royal jelly capsules!

Despite the fact that the capsules are meant to be taken internally, some ingenious people have used them in other ways to good effect. A Cumbrian enthusiast split open a capsule and applied the contents to a troublesome cold sore. He said 'I was amazed how quickly my cold sore cleared up! (A noticeable improvement in about five hours in fact!)'

What is in them?

You will find that most capsules contain 100 – 500 mg of royal jelly: the optimum dosage is 150 mg. Usually, the substance is mixed with other ingredients such as soya bean oil, hydrogenated vegetable oil, beeswax, soya lecithin and other plant extracts. The coating of these capsules is generally made of gelatin.

Remember when you are shopping around for capsules to look for ones which contain *fresh* royal jelly, if possible preserved in honey and wheatgerm oil, since these are the most effective preservatives. Such capsules may seem expensive, but when you think about the price, it is the equivalent per month of a cheap restaurant meal or a seat at the theatre. The cost also compares favourably with that of a visit to the hairdresser, or a jar of top-quality face cream. By the time you have been taking the capsules for a few months, your hair and skin will be in such good condition that you will probably be saving money in that department anyway.

Part of the reason for the relatively high cost of fresh royal jelly capsules is that, in addition to the fact that fresh royal jelly is dear, the technology required to preserve and encapsulate this very volatile substance in its fresh state is itself expensive. However, almost all those who have tried both the freeze-dried and the fresh versions are more than happy to pay the extra money for those extra benefits which they derive from fresh royal jelly.

How can you tell whether the capsules are working?

It is often the case that, when people start taking royal jelly capsules, an improvement in their general health occurs so gradually that they begin to wonder whether it is worth carrying on taking them. One lady from Edinburgh came to just that conclusion.

I took the capsules for 3 months and noticed no amazing transformation in myself. I was then away on holiday and had taken no supply with me. When I returned I had lost the habit of the daily dose, and in the following weeks I lost the glow and zest which had crept up on me so subtly that I hadn't realized the benefits which that tiny capsule had given me.

My skin and hair protested, and my nails split and flaked. I'm glad to say that I'm now re-established on my routine of the 'golden glow'.

A Middlesex sceptic had a similar experience.

I stopped taking royal jelly thinking it had not worked in any way. It was when my hairdresser commented that my hair and nail growth had dramatically slowed down that I immediately started taking royal jelly again.

From having a negative attitude towards royal jelly, I am now positive that it works. Today my hair and nails, tomorrow who knows!

The moral of these tales is that, even if you cannot notice any improvement, give the capsules time and try to remember how you were before you started taking them. It would be a good idea to keep a diary for a few months so that you can monitor your progress and have a more objective view, with hindsight, of the effectiveness of royal jelly. If you are still unconvinced, stop taking the capsules for a few weeks — I can guarantee that you will notice the difference, as the benefits slowly accrued over the months evaporate within a week or two!

—————— Royal jelly with honey ——————

Royal jelly and honey products are invaluable for three groups of people: vegetarians, who cannot take capsules because of the gelatin casing; the very young, who have not yet learned how to swallow a capsule; and anyone, including the very elderly, who experiences difficulty in swallowing pills or capsules.

As with the capsules, you will find a wide variation in the prices of these products. This is not because some hold freeze-dried royal jelly while others contain the fresh variety since, as honey is one of the easiest ways of preserving royal jelly, most contain the fresh substance. However, there *is* a difference in the proportion of royal jelly, so you would do well to check the labels carefully before buying. Look out for a product which will provide 150 mg of fresh royal jelly per teaspoonful, as this is the optimum daily dosage. If the quantity of royal jelly is not marked, steer clear — it probably means that there is merely a 'token' amount.

In addition to honey, these royal jelly products usually contain bee pollen and vitamin C, a really palatable and vitalizing mixture! The sweetness of royal jelly with honey makes it a delicious breakfast time spread, or it can even be taken from a spoon, so it is a really easy and pleasant way for all the family to take their daily dose of royal jelly. The one thing you should *not* do is add the product to a hot drink as this will destroy the beneficial properties of the royal jelly.

I recently received a letter about a typical royal jelly and honey family from a mum in Rutland.

I have two small children of 5 and 3 years and have started giving them a spoonful every morning and the benefits are most noticeable. The eldest was finding it difficult to cope with school until he started the honey — he now has the energy to last the day and is less prone to throw his hands up and admit defeat so easily. . . he has managed to remain cold-free despite the sneezes and snuffles going round school. With the little girl the benefits are more pronounced — to put it bluntly, she is a little ratbag without her daily spoonful. We ran out of the honey one Friday and the weekend was dreadful with her tantrums and arguments. After a few days back on the honey she was back to her cheerful and less tired outlook.

I also have a spoonful every morning and it certainly helps me. I seem to have more energy to cope with the children and the driving job I have. In fact I take a jar with me and when I find myself flagging I have another spoonful!

Liquid royal jelly tonic

For a really fast-acting 'pick-me-up' there is nothing to beat royal jelly tonic. The tonic consists of fresh royal jelly, mixed with several other energizing ingredients, and it is packaged in single-dose phials. Many people find that the tonic begins to work within minutes, giving an energizing effect which lasts throughout the day, while others find a gradual increase in their energy levels until a stable peak is reached. Whatever the case, the boost given to sluggish systems is dramatic.

Strangely, this injection of energy does not prevent you from sleeping when the time comes, despite the fact that you feel as though you could keep going for ever. A Northampton lady, who was already taking royal jelly capsules daily, put the tonic to the test.

I had been to two parties on consecutive nights; the first party ended at 4.30 am, the second at 6 am. On the third night I was faced with yet another party which I knew would also last well into the next day. I felt like death — and looked like it, I may add. The thought of going anywhere but bed had me contemplating suicide!! To the amusement of my husband, children and babysitter, I drank the liquid tonic. I went to the party, I danced all night, had a wonderful time and got to bed at 4.30 am. Now, if that wasn't *the* test, I don't know what is!

Even later in life, when we expect to be able to sit back and watch the grass grow, there are still days when we need an energy booster. Mrs B. from Macclesfield writes,

Last week I had need to do a very strenuous few days of driving — 900 miles in three days. When I arrived back home at 9.15p.m. my friends volunteered how fresh I looked, showing no signs of expected strain at my age of 70 years! Then I told them I had taken just one small teaspoonful of liquid royal jelly tonic for each of the last three mornings. 'No wonder!' they said.

When you look at what these liquid pick-me-ups contain, it is hardly surprising that they have such a dramatic effect. The most effective kind contains 50 per cent fresh royal jelly — approximately 0.5 g, or up to five times as much royal jelly as is contained in some capsules. It is perfectly all right to take this quantity of royal jelly when a special energy boost is required, but I would not recommend anyone to take 0.5 g every day. That is not to say that such a daily dose has been shown to cause any serious side-effects.

However, you may find that you have rather more energy than is desirable! In any event, such a dosage taken on a daily basis is simply not necessary. The royal jelly is blended with honey, which adds to the energizing capacity of the tonic, as well as ginseng, plant extracts of *damiana aphrodisiaca* and saw palmetto, a trace of capsicum and almond essence.

Ginseng is extracted from the roots of the plant *Panax ginseng* (see Fig 6) and is probably most famous for its role in increasing sexual appetites, but it is also effective in fighting depression and fatigue, resulting in a boost in both physical and mental energy. The Chinese, of course, have used ginseng for thousands of years in their medicines, and Russian cosmonauts have used it too to increase their resistance to stress and fatigue.

Incidentally, both ginseng and *damiana aphrodisiaca* are believed to relieve some of the unpleasant symptoms experienced during the menopause, Ginseng, in particular, contains estriol, a form of oestrogen, so there would seem to be a scientific basis for its helpfulness during the menopause, when a lack of oestrogen produces so many unpleasant symptoms.

However, I should point out that the liquid royal jelly tonic is not intended to be taken every day; far from it. Rather it has been formulated as a supplement to the daily capsule, to be used only occasionally, when you are planning to undertake unusually strenuous physical or mental activity.

Fig 6   Ginseng

Skincare

One of the first results noticed by those who take fresh royal jelly is that the condition of their skin, nails and hair improves dramatically. It was therefore a logical step to try applying royal jelly externally to skin rashes and lesions. The outcome was very encouraging so, a few years ago, one of the first skin creams containing this effective salve was produced.

Royal jelly & vitamin E cream

The most successful of these royal jelly creams is blended with vitamin E, as well as jojoba oil and beeswax. When taken internally, vitamin E has a longstanding reputation for protecting cells as they divide and multiply. More recently, its role when used in ointments to help heal ulcers, burns and cuts has been highlighted. As such, this vitamin has similar properties to royal jelly, and the combination of these two active ingredients has produced some remarkable results.

It was initially intended that royal jelly cream be used on the face and neck, but many purchasers tried it on other parts of their body with considerable success, For example, a concert pianist has discovered that the cream can even safeguard his livelihood.

My finger tips, which were often chapped and cracked, particularly in cold weather, have completely healed and are no longer giving me any trouble. Having to play the piano in recitals and when teaching I have for years suffered much pain and frustration which has now completely disappeared.

As you will discover in Chapter 7, both royal jelly & vitamin E cream and royal jelly capsules can have dramatic effects on severe eczema, psoriasis and other skin conditions. One lady achieved startling results when she used the cream on a cyst. She had consulted her doctor who told her that she would have to have it excised when it became uncomfortable. Although the lump on her wrist was already painful, since my correspondent was about to go on holiday she decided to wait until she returned before seeing a specialist. I shall let her take up the story.

The lump got bigger and bigger and was making my arm ache as well, so I thought I would try rubbing some of the cream on it morning and evening. This I did for a while and then one morning I woke up and found the lump had gone right down. Then the lump started to come again a week ago so once again I have been putting the cream on and the lump has gone down again!

Fortunately, most of us are free from such worrying complaints, but still we can derive great benefit from the soothing and revitalizing properties of the cream. A happy lady from Surrey says, 'After using royal jelly & vitamin E cream for about three months. . . friends, relatives — even the beauty consultants at various stores — have all commented on my skin, saying how it glows.' Another lady had found that her skin reacted to all the creams she had tried in the past: 'Everything I tried only made my itchy, sensitive skin that much worse. However, after a day out in the frosty cold my skin was so sore and flaky. I tried the cream and found to my surprise how soothing it was — and no itching!'

An even more recent development than royal jelly & vitamin E skin cream is the appearance on the market of complete skincare ranges containing royal jelly. By way of a warning, some of the cheap brands have minute quantities of the freeze-dried product simply so that the words 'royal jelly' can be used on the packaging.

However, there is one range in particular which uses a significant proportion of pure, fresh royal jelly. The price inevitably reflects the fresh royal jelly content, but at least you know that the products will give your skin the maximum benefits. I should state that I played a considerable part in helping to formulate the range: I knew from my own experience how beneficial royal jelly is to the skin and many of my correspondents had expressed the hope that such a range might be developed. Modern skincare formulations are more like a list of chemicals than a careful blending of natural ingredients, but this new range seems to make the most of what nature has to offer, with no animal-derived ingredients in its constituents. The range at present comprises a cleansing bar, cleansing lotion, skin tonic, moisturizer, night cream, eye gel and face mask.

Cleansing bar

This is the ideal cleanser if you prefer washing your face to using a lotion. Its balanced pH avoids the drastic changes which occur in the acid-alkali balance of your skin when you wash with soap-based cleansers. This very gentle cleansing bar contains fresh royal jelly, our old friend vitamin E, plant extracts and essential oils.

Cleansing lotion

For those who have very dry skin, the cleansing lotion is preferable. This revitalizing, light, non-greasy lotion removes all traces of make-up and grime, but at the same time gives your skin the benefits of fresh royal jelly, vitamin E, plant extracts and essential oils — a real feast for your epidermis!

Skin tonic

Toning refreshes the skin by helping to close the pores and refine the oilier areas over the forehead, nose and chin. As well as fresh royal jelly, the revitalizing skin tonic contains gammalinolenic acid-rich oil, vitamin E, menthol plant extracts, essential oils and roseflower extract. There is no alcohol in the formulation which will be a great relief to anyone with a sensitive skin.

Moisturizer

Moisturizing the skin after toning is an essential part of any skincare routine, and the light, non-clogging royal jelly moisturizer is full of good things to nourish as well as moisturize the skin. Rosehip oil, carrot oil, GLA-rich oils, soothing allantoin and beeswax combine with royal jelly and vitamin E. There is even a light sunscreen, although it is recommended that additional sunscreen be used when sunbathing.

Night cream

This is even richer and more nourishing than the moisturizer and contains the biggest percentage of royal jelly of all the products in the range. As well as essential oils, it has vitamins E and A which are both known to improve skin condition.

Eye gel

The skin around your eyes is extremely sensitive and we should be very wary about slapping on the first cream that comes to hand. However, this gel has nothing in it which could irritate or harm the delicate tissues — on the contrary, it contains royal jelly and, once again, vitamin E, as well as other natural ingredients such as soothing aloe vera.

Face mask

The best gentle but revitalizing face masks draw impurities out of the skin as well as moisturizing and nourishing it, and this one has the right mix of ingredients to carry out the task effectively. Royal jelly and vitamin E are combined with natural moisturizers in a creamy clay base and I use this excellent product regularly, once or twice a week.

These products have a natural, delicate fragrance which comes solely from the essential oils and plant extracts which have been included in the formulation because of their own intrinsic beneficial properties.

I can say with confidence that the products in this skincare range are perfectly safe for all skins, which cannot be claimed for some of the skin preparations I have used in the past. If your skin is sensitive, you will know what I mean. You will suffer from, for example, redness, blotchy patches, itchiness and rashes. It never ceases to amaze me that we are expected to pay good money for products which leave our skin in a worse state than it was before we applied them! I can vouch from my own experience for the reliability and effectiveness of these royal jelly skin products. I use them as a matter of course and my skin really feels the benefit.

All the products in the royal jelly skincare range have undergone unusually thorough and expensive testing — on people, not on animals. The night cream, which is richest in the active ingredients, was tested under full supervision on 100 volunteers, not one of whom showed an allergic or negative response. Indeed, several groups of cosmetic products were tested during that series of trials, and the fresh royal jelly range put many of the others to shame! Given the natural ingredients and absence of known allergens or irritants in these products, such a result was only to be expected.

It will be interesting to see whether these skincare products have similar effects to the royal jelly cream. There is every reason to believe they will, but it is early days yet and only time will tell.

P.S.

There is a fascinating postscript to the development of this skincare range. Vicki Dryden-Wyatt, a well-known freelance cosmetics consultant, assisted in the formulation of these products. When Vicki was first asked to work on the project she was an 'absolute cynic' about the value of fresh royal jelly. She had heard about enough 'miracle' products in her walk of life to take any claims with a very large pinch of salt. Then, on her first visit to the company, Vicki was shown their range of fresh royal jelly products and tasted a little of each, including the tonic. She left the office with samples of all the company's products, but with no change in her opinion on royal jelly.

'That night,' said Vicki, 'I didn't get home until about one o'clock in the morning. Surprisingly, I wasn't feeling at all tired, so I worked on until five o'clock. I didn't connect my newfound energy with the tonic at all.'

A few days later, Vicki had a busy evening ahead of her and decided to take a phial of the liquid royal jelly tonic before she left home, to see whether it would have any effect. 'Again, I returned home at one o'clock and worked through until dawn. It was only when I had finished work that I thought back and realized that it was thanks to the royal jelly tonic that I had felt so wide awake and full of energy on both occasions.'

Needless to say, Vicki has been taking her daily royal jelly capsule ever since, with occasional phials of tonic for extra energy. 'And I intend to carry on taking that brand of fresh royal jelly', said Vicki, firmly. 'I can definitely say that my energy levels are higher because of royal jelly. My skin, hair and nails have improved too.'

As so often happens, the royal jelly habit has spread through Vicki's family. Her husband, who is a down-to-earth farmer, decided to give the capsules a try. 'After just two weeks he noticed that he felt more energetic, too', reported Vicki. 'This may sound mad,' she went on, 'but, you know, he was bald on top and now his hair has started to grow back!'

I have so many instances of experiences like Vicki's: stories of people who begin by being totally cynical about the effects of fresh royal jelly but who, once they have tried it, become lifelong converts and fervent evangelists.

Whatever next?

It will be fascinating to see what new royal jelly products come on to the market over the next few years. If the Chinese experience is anything to go by, there is plenty of room for expansion. During my trip to China I saw a complete counter devoted to royal jelly and other bee products in the 'Friendship Shop' in Beijing. Given the fact that the East has a revered tradition of natural medicine I should not have been surprised, but some of the products left me speechless. To give just a few examples, I saw crystallized royal jelly, royal jelly chocolate, royal jelly wine — even royal jelly talcum powder!

It may be tempting to scoff at such products, but the West is only now beginning to appreciate Eastern values and Eastern wisdom in all realms of life, from abstract philosophy to practical scientific knowledge. I also feel that we, in a society dominated by materialism, junk food and the soap opera, are hardly in a position to pour scorn on beliefs and practices rooted in a respect for nature and spiritual values.

Be that as it may, whether we shall see royal jelly chocolate and wine taking the West by storm, only time will tell! Nevertheless, I am convinced that there is ample scope in the West for new royal jelly products, and I shall watch such developments with interest.

CHAPTER 4

— The Chinese connection —

Some years ago I discovered that the best royal jelly in the world comes from China and from that moment on I was determined to visit the country to see for myself how the Chinese produce such high-quality royal jelly. As soon as I began making enquiries I realized that arranging such a trip would not be without its problems. The Chinese government proved very wary about letting a Westerner observe its production methods, let alone photograph or film them, and for some time I thought I would never make the journey.

However, one day I had the idea of contacting Lord Ennals, since I knew that both he and his wife were great royal jelly enthusiasts. I therefore wrote to ask him if he would be kind enough to intercede on my behalf with the Chinese government. To my great fortune, the Labour peer was a friend of the Chinese Ambassador to the United Kingdom and, within a very short time of my request, I found that all the doors which had previously been closed to me were flung wide open. So it was that in July 1987 I became the first Westerner to witness and film the Chinese method of extracting royal jelly. Before I chronicle this fascinating trip, I should like to provide you with some background on China's position as world leader in royal jelly production and export.

Although beekeeping has a very long history, in the West it has become a booming commercial industry only over the last century. Even then, most bees are kept for their honey, rather than for the royal jelly they produce. The picture of commercial beekeeping and royal jelly production in China, however, is rather different.

There is evidence to show that the Chinese have been bee-keepers for more than 3,000 years, using their native honey bee, *Apis Cerana* (the 'wax bee'). Indeed the Chinese word for honey has been found in inscriptions on bones dating from 1400–1000 BC in the form of an ancient Chinese pictograph. Later records of honey bees can be found in the earliest collections of poetry, the *Book of Songs* (800–100 BC), and in the first etiquette manual, the

Book of Rites (100 BC). The Chinese for 'honey' and 'bee' appear in the earliest extant dictionary dating from 100 AD, and the *Book on Chinese Medicine* (*c.* 220 BC) describes honey as a very beneficial medicine. Moving on through history, medical and agricultural books written in the 11th century describe beekeeping practices in considerable detail. It seems that, at that time, bees were kept in wooden tubs and bamboo cages.

At the dawn of the 20th century, the western bee, *Apis Mellifera* (the 'honey bee'), was imported into China but still, shortly before the establishment of the People's Republic of China in 1949, there were fewer than half a million colonies and their total annual honey yield was a mere 8,000 tonnes.

With the revolution in social organization there came a revolution in Chinese attitudes to beekeeping. Less than forty years later, there are now about 6 million domesticated colonies producing more than 100,000 tonnes of honey a year. The most startling statistic, however, is that for royal jelly production — in excess of 600 tonnes annually! This figure is far ahead of any other country's output.

The reason for this 'intensive farming' of royal jelly in China is clear enough. As we saw in Chapter 3, the Chinese, more than any other race, have realized the benefits of royal jelly and use it in a very wide range of products. Indeed, less than one-third of the total Chinese royal jelly production is exported, the remainder being used in medicines and in the wide variety of royal jelly products available on the domestic market.

The importance attached to beekeeping as a whole in China is demonstrated by the fact that their Ministry of Agriculture, Animal Husbandry and Fisheries has a special department responsible for apiculture in most provinces. Its officers organize apicultural production, advise on the distribution of the various plants from which the bees extract nectar for honey-making, and they also design programmes for boosting production.

In 1958, the Institute of Apicultural Research of the Chinese Academy of Agricultural Sciences was established in Beijing. It now has a staff of 120, including 70 postgraduate researchers. The Institute plans scientific development in apiculture and co-ordinates research projects throughout the country. Some agricultural universities offer degree courses in apiculture and studies can be pursued up to doctorate level.

Given the State's wholehearted commitment to apiculture, it is hardly surprising that China has such a large output of hive products. That being said, most Chinese apiaries are small, ranging in size from 50 to 80 colonies, although at the other end of the spectrum you can find large-scale apiaries with hundreds of thousands of colonies.

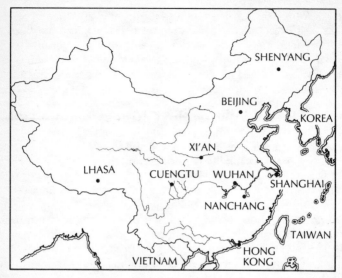

Fig 7 Fragrance Mountain is situated near Beijing, location of the Institute of Apicultural Research of the Chinese Academy of Agricultural Sciences.

On average, each beekeeper looks after 30 colonies, harvesting honey, royal jelly, pollen and propolis from his hives. In some areas, up to 2 kg of royal jelly is produced annually by each honey-bee colony.

Of course, annual yields depend not only on hive management methods, but also on the climate, and it must be remembered that China covers 9.6 million sq km, from very cold to tropical zones. Since the 1950s, to make the best of this wide range of climatic conditions, beekeepers and their colonies have migrated long distances by special trains, following the plant pollination season around the country.

The sub-tropical and tropical regions are the main areas for *Apis mellifera* colonies. The majority of these Western honey bees are the Italian strain, *Apis ligustica*, for reasons which I explained in Chapter 1. In contrast, the native Chinese bee, *Apis cerana*, can be found all over the country, particularly in the south-west and south. Over the years, these bees have adapted to the most rigorous conditions and have become very hardy.

As I have already mentioned, in earlier times Chinese bees were kept in round wooden buckets, but the annual honey yield per colony using this method was only about 5 kg per colony. As a result, movable-frame hives were introduced, increasing the yield to 15–20 kg per colony per year.

As you would expect, China produces many different kinds of honey, including jujuba, litchi, milk vetch, acacia and lime. This honey is purchased and resold by the State, most of it being supplied to medical factories and combined with Chinese herbs for the manufacture of traditional remedies. Some is also supplied to food factories for sweets, cakes and candied fruit or is bottled in food factories for sale in shops. In addition, 30,000 – 40,000 tonnes are exported annually.

——————Royal jelly — the Chinese way——————

During my fascinating trip to China in July 1987, I was fortunate enough to see for myself how the hives at the Fragrance Mountain Research Institute of Chinese Apiculture are managed, and how royal jelly is produced and preserved there. This beautiful corner of China is the centre of much of the world's apicultural research work, so I was able to investigate the latest developments in royal jelly production.

I have always believed that Chinese fresh royal jelly is of superior quality, and what I discovered confirmed my belief. In many other countries, beekeepers who practise intensive royal jelly production feed their bees with a sugar and water solution, and the quality of the royal jelly thus produced is markedly affected. In China, however, bees are never fed such solutions; their only source of food is the wide variety of flowering plants which abound in that country.

Fig 8 Fragrance Mountain

Fragrance Mountain is carpeted with flowers which are rich in nectar and pollen. The way these plants are cultivated is important, since there can be slight differences in the royal jelly according to the nutrition of the plants from which nectar and pollen are gathered.

The average number of bees in each of the 130 colonies at the bee farm on Fragrance Mountain is 33,000, but the structure of their hives would surprise any traditional beekeeper. Inside each hive is a specially designed frame. This frame usually supports 80 artificial 'queen cups', although it can take as many as 145. At one time, these artifical cups were made of wax, but nowadays they tend to be made of plastic. (Recent research has, in fact, proved that the amount of royal jelly collected from plastic cups exceeds that collected from the traditional beeswax versions.) The artificial queen cups hang vertically, rather than horizontally, on the frame (see Fig 9). The direction in which they lie is crucial, for in nature only cups which contain larvae destined to be queens are laid out in this configuration As a result, the worker bees are tricked into believing that they are nourishing queens and they therefore deliver royal jelly to the larvae in these cells in greater quantity and in a more concentrated form. The small worker bee larvae are gently transferred into these cups and then this section of 80 – 100 cups is attached to a frame and lowered into the hive.

Research has shown that the best time to collect royal jelly from the artificial cups is 72 hours after the frame has been introduced

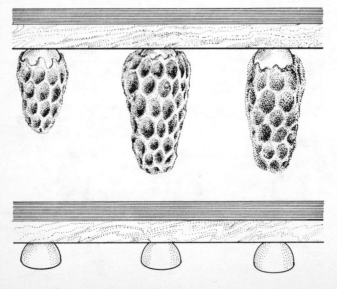

Fig 9 Artificial queen cup frame

into the hive. The Chinese have arrived at this figure for three reasons. The most important is that after three days the quality of the royal jelly is at its peak. Secondly, they have discovered that, after three days, the maximum amount of royal jelly is present in the cups. By this stage, the jelly is thicker in consistency and can no longer be ingested by the larvae. The third reason is that, as soon as the workers discover the cups, they not only begin to feed the larvae inside with royal jelly, but they also begin to deposit wax on the rim of the cups. Within five days the cups will be completely sealed and, less than a week later, the new queens will have emerged.

So, three days after the introduction of the frame, the staff of the Research Institute's bee farm remove the frame and take it indoors to cut away the beeswax deposits. Then the larvae are taken out of their royal jelly beds. Finally, the royal jelly is collected from the cups by syphoning it through a filter into a special bottle. Each cup can be expected to yield 0.3 g of royal jelly. Once the bottle is full, it is sealed and refrigerated to ensure that its contents are kept fresh and do not deteriorate. The production process then starts all over again. New larvae are introduced into the artificial queen cups before the frame is replaced in the hive.

The Chinese obtain a phenomenal success rate using this method: on the frame I inspected, 76 of the 80 queen cups contained royal jelly, so the worker bees really do think that they are feeding queens! (At this point I must stress that at no stage in the entire process are the bees harmed in any way.)

The highest annual production from any one bee colony using artificial queen frames is 2 kg per year. However, this applies only to southern China where there is a long harvesting season. In the colder northern part of the country, the royal jelly production season is restricted by the climate to May – August, so output is considerably reduced, to approximately 0.5 kg per colony.

Breeding 'super bees'

One of the many other fascinating areas of research work at Fragrance Mountain is the selective bee-breeding programme, designed to meet the increasingly large demand for royal jelly and other bee products.

I felt very honoured in being allowed to watch the workings of this programme in another research block on Fragrance Mountain. Here the researchers were hard at work breeding queen bees to develop a strain which will produce only the best royal jelly. The basis for this research is the Italian bee, which has proved such a friend to honey and royal jelly producers around the world.

The initial phase of the breeding cycle involves selecting individual drones to fertilize the queens. A great deal of 'in-breeding' goes on, since the drones are usually the offspring of the queens they will inseminate: this has been shown to improve the quality of the eventual bee products. All the bees used in the programme are from the Italian strain, both because they produce a better quality of royal jelly and because they are less likely to sting the researchers! The process of collecting donor sperm from the drones is an extremely delicate one requiring the latest microsurgery techniques.

Once the sperm has been collected, the task of artificially inseminating the queen is begun. She is sedated (with no harmful after-effects, I hasten to add) and is then inserted gently into the neck of a small tube, which holds her immobile. The sperm is then introduced into the queen bee, and the larvae which emerge from her eggs are later placed in special queen cells.

The breeding programme uses the same artificial queen cells which are used in royal jelly production, but in this case only 40 cups are used on each frame and the larvae are left alone in the hives until they hatch into queens.

It is only by close observation of the offspring of the new queen bee, examining the quality and quantity of the royal jelly produced by her worker bee children, that researchers can evaluate the success of their work. Consequently, improving the strain is a slow, laborious task, but the Chinese have great hope for the future and, fortunately, they are a very patient people!

CHAPTER 5

Fresh or freeze-dried: what's the difference?

During my Chinese trip I was particularly interested in the methods they use to preserve royal jelly. As you will have gathered by now, I firmly believe that fresh royal jelly, properly preserved, is infinitely preferable to the freeze-dried variety. It was therefore with great satisfaction that I learned from my hosts on Fragrance Mountain that royal jelly produced on the bee farm is refrigerated.

In that part of China the daytime temperature regularly rises to 30°C (86°F) and often higher. In such conditions, royal jelly is unlikely to survive outside the hive for more than a day without spoiling. I was therefore curious to know how royal jelly was preserved by those Chinese who did not own refrigerators. It transpired that many people in that country preserve their fresh royal jelly by plunging it in cold water or burying it in the earth (see Fig 10) to keep its temperature down to approximately 12°C (52°F). Even this is not quite cool enough, and the royal jelly has to be consumed within three days.

The optimum storage temperature for fresh royal jelly, in the opinion of my Chinese hosts who are the acknowledged experts, is between 5°C (41°F) and −5°C (23°F) which accords with my experience. Interestingly, they also accept storage of royal jelly at −15°C (5°F) if it has to be kept for a long time. This, of course, is well below the temperature at which royal jelly freezes, but it should be stressed that the Chinese do *not* recommend freeze-drying royal jelly, a process which both removes all the moisture content and affects the chemical structure of the substance. None of the elements is actually lost, but the molecules which make up the substance become rearranged to form new structures. The most important alteration during this process is the degradation of the amino acids, and you will have gathered from Chapter 2 that these acids are vital to royal jelly's performance in many areas.

Many people have told me that they, too, believe from their own experience that fresh royal jelly is infinitely superior to the freeze-dried variety. For instance, Katie Boyle says, 'I have tried both, and

Fig 10 Burying royal jelly in the earth

I'm sure that the dried variety is less effective than the fresh.'
Another user of fresh royal jelly told me, 'It is certainly far more
effective than any of the freeze-dried royal jellies I have used
before.'

When royal jelly products first appeared on the Western market,
they were all freeze-dried. This was mainly because no one thought
it possible to find a way of preserving royal jelly long enough for it to
be shipped, stored in warehouses and then kept on shop shelves
without freeze-drying it. Eventually a solution *was* found. It involved preserving the fresh royal jelly in honey and wheatgerm oil,
then encapsulating it in gelatin. The resulting capsules had a shelf
life of three years which is more than adequate. Incidentally, during
the search for an efficient preservative, vegetable oil was tested but
found inferior to wheatgerm oil. I would therefore advise anyone

wanting to obtain the best royal jelly capsules to look closely at the labels before deciding which brand to buy and to eschew any which contain vegetable oil rather than honey and wheatgerm oil as a preservative.

Developing a process to bring fresh royal jelly to the consumer in exactly the form in which it was taken from the hive was a long, painstaking task and many people may wonder whether it was worth the effort and the expense. Are we perhaps obsessed with the idea that the words 'pure', 'fresh', 'natural' or 'unprocessed' must mean that the product they describe is actually better than its processed equivalent?

Of course, freeze-drying (or lyophilization, as it is technically called) is a simple way of preserving royal jelly for long periods and, because of this, you will find that freeze-dried royal jelly is considerably cheaper than the fresh, but unfortunately it does seem to be much less potent. When you think about other examples of freeze-drying, this deterioration is not surprising. For instance, I defy anyone to state in all sincerity that freeze-dried coffee has exactly the same flavour as freshly ground coffee.

Even in the earliest days of my involvement with royal jelly I was convinced that the fresh product was vastly superior. However, convictions which are based on opinion rather than fact carry very little weight, so I decided to investigate the scientific literature. Relatively early on in my search I came across a fascinating paper written by scientists from the Department of Agriculture at the University of Bologna. Their work revealed that two elements in fresh royal jelly are degraded in the freeze-drying process, the sugars and the amino acids. The result of degrading the sugars is an alteration in flavour (detectable as a slightly 'roasted' taste). Although the degradation of amino acids cannot be identified by taste it seemed to me to be a disastrous side-effect of the lyophilization process. I decided to investigate further.

A Polish paper, dauntingly titled '*Amino acid composition of hydrolyzates of fresh and lyophilized royal jelly*,' shed more light on the subject. It states that 'there were significant differences between fresh and lyophilized royal jelly in the contents of lysine, serine, alanine and isoleucine (*all amino acids*), and also of sugar.'

The Poles' analysis revealed a significant reduction in the quantity of isoleucine present in the lyophilized royal jelly, but an increase in the lysine, serine and alanine content (along with a virtual 100 per cent increase in the sugar content!). Now serine and alanine can be manufactured by the body, but we have to synthesize isoleucine and lysine from the food we eat. Of all the amino acids in royal jelly, aspartic acid (which our bodies can manufacture) is present in the greatest quantity, with isoleucine coming a close second. Perhaps it is this significantly greater amount of isoleucine which accounts for the superiority of fresh over freeze-dried royal jelly. As yet, no firm conclusions have been reached.

However, during my research I came across some fascinating work carried out in the late 1970s in Egypt. In their paper, *'Royal Jelly — a Revelation or a Fable?'*, which appeared in the *Egyptian Journal of Veterinary Science*, Salama, Mogawar and El-Tohamy experimented with the comparative effect of fresh and freeze-dried royal jelly on immature rats. Here, at last, was some scientific research which bore directly on my quest!

Before I go any further, I should like to reassure those readers who might disagree with experimenting on animals. As you will have gathered by now, royal jelly has no toxic effects whatsoever — after all, it is a wholly natural food.

The results of the Egyptian experiments were startling, to say the least. There were 210 female immature rats in the trial. These were divided into seven groups of 30 receiving the following quantities of royal jelly daily for four weeks.

Group 1   10 mg fresh royal jelly
Group 2   20 mg fresh royal jelly
Group 3   40 mg fresh royal jelly

Group 4   10 mg freeze-dried royal jelly
Group 5   20 mg freeze-dried royal jelly
Group 6   40 mg freeze-dried royal jelly

Group 7   0.5 ml distilled water.
(control group)

Every daily dose of royal jelly was diluted in 0.5 ml distilled water to make sure that any effects observed were not produced by the water rather than the royal jelly!

The rats were weighed each week and, in the third week, they were taken to fertile rats by night and returned to their special cages by day until the end of the experiment.

Later on, when it was obvious that a female was pregnant, she was isolated until she gave birth. The pups were counted when they were born and the scientists calculated the date of fertilization by counting back from the date of birth.

At the beginning of the experiment, the rats all weighed within 1 g of 37 g. At the end of the experiment, the average weight of each group was as follows:

Group 1   64.1 g
Group 2   74.4 g
Group 3   78.8 g

Group 4   59.0 g
Group 5   65.9 g
Group 6   71.4 g

Group 7   59.7 g.

The figures speak for themselves don't they? Simply compare those for Group 3 (40 mg fresh royal jelly), Group 6 (40 mg freeze-dried royal jelly) and Group 7 (the control group, taking distilled water only). After just four weeks, the rats fed on fresh royal jelly had streaked ahead not only of those given distilled water, but also of those given freeze-dried royal jelly! What is more, the figures for weekly growth reflect the same trend. These figures are easier to absorb when they are converted into chart form (see Fig 11).

As the Egyptian scientists themselves conclude, 'Fresh royal jelly is more potent than the lyophilized material dispensed to commerce, a fact which indicates that the process of preservation and lyophilization affected in some way the activity and potency of the material.'

But there was more to come. 'Concerning maturity, the results were very amazing: considering that the date of successful fertilization is the actual time of maturity, the results show that Group 3 (40 mg fresh royal jelly) reached maturity 26 days from the beginning of treatment — 16 days earlier than the control group. The date of maturity was related to the dose administered and the growth rate' (see Fig 12).

Even those rats given just 10 mg per day of fresh royal jelly matured 4 days before the control group, whereas those given 40 mg of freeze-dried royal jelly matured only 12 days before the control group, compared with 26 days of the 40 mg fresh royal jelly group. This effect is demonstrated clearly in the bar chart.

The scientists did point out that this early maturity might have been due to a general improvement in the condition of the rats through taking royal jelly, rather than to any direct effect which royal jelly may have on maturity, but they conceded that, whatever the case, the resulting effects were the same!

Perhaps you are wondering whether giving fresh royal jelly to your children will result in their putting on weight and reaching puberty well before they reach their teens. I can put your mind to rest on both scores.

To begin with, we have to bear in mind that the recommended adult daily dose of fresh royal jelly is 150 mg. This may well be almost four times the maximum dose given to the immature rats, but compare body weights! If a 40 kg youngster were to take the equivalent of a 40 mg dose for a 40 g rat, he would have to take 4 kg of royal jelly per day, and that would be 26,666 150 mg capsules!

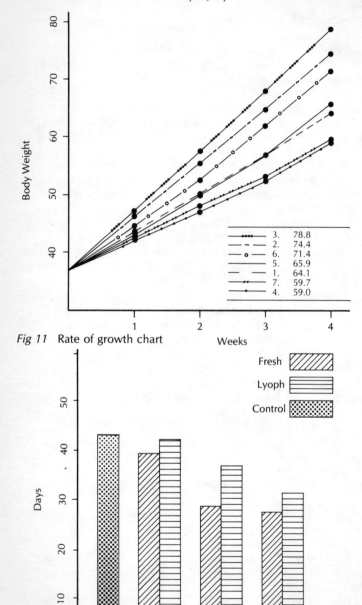

Fig 11   Rate of growth chart

Fig 12   Maturity dates graph

It is clear that the effect of royal jelly is proportionate to the quantity taken. The larva destined to become a queen bee consumes nothing but royal jelly, and we saw in Chapter 1 what that did for her! The rats were all on the same normal diet with the royal jelly being given as a supplement, so the effect on them was somewhat less dramatic.

The human recommended daily dose of 150mg has been arrived at by experience and has been calculated to give a sustained improvement in general health and well-being.

With regard to putting on weight, the paper referred to an experiment which Salama and Mogawar had carried out earlier in 1977. This had shown that, when royal jelly was given to old rats (who rather like some elderly humans had become somewhat obese due to relative inactivity), they lost weight. The scientists concluded that 'this reduction was attributable to an increased metabolic rate to meet the increased energy demands. In this work [*the trial on immature rats*], we found that although the vitality of the growing rats was much increased, the growth rate was highly promoted.'

Here we have yet more evidence of the 'balancing' effect of royal jelly. The rats which needed to put on weight did so, while those which needed to lose it did so, too.

Unfortunately, very little scientific work is being done in English-speaking countries on the comparative virtues of fresh and freeze-dried royal jelly, so we have to rely on studies such as the one I have just quoted. This is not to detract from its validity, since all the requirements of the scientific world were met, including strict supervision and the provision of control subjects. At the same time, given the amount of scientific investigation which is being carried out in the rest of the world, particularly in China and the Eastern bloc, it is a shame that the scientific establishment in the West, with its greater resources and more advanced technologies, cannot pick up the gauntlet thrown down by those who truly believe in the beneficial effects of fresh royal jelly and initiate full-scale research.

——A picture is worth a thousand words——

Some very interesting research work *has* been carried out in Britain, however. In December 1987, the most potent brand of fresh royal jelly was compared with a cheaper 'fresh' version and a freeze-dried brand. The technique used for this experiment was Kirlian photography.

Kirlian photography is a method of recording the electro-magnetic radiation emission of objects on photographic emulsion. Although electro-photography was first invented in 1842, the technique was not widely accepted until 1958, when two Russian scientists, Semyon and Valentina Kirlian, released photographs they had taken using this method.

As usual with Eastern scientific developments, the West was somewhat sceptical in the beginning, but by 1970 the technique had begun to attract followers in Europe and America. In 1975, Kendall Johnson wrote a book called *The Living Aura* and this created even more interest in Kirlian photography.

What are these electro-magnetic emissions? Some researchers believe that they are a reflection of 'bio-energy', or the 'life flux'. When workers took photographs of leaves and small animals, they found that living things produced a much clearer and highly contrasted image than their dead counterparts. For example, photographs of a leaf taken over a period of time revealed that the bio-energy diminished in size and intensity as the leaf began to die. Another interesting discovery was that, when a portion of the leaf was torn off, a photograph of the remaining part still showed the missing portion as a 'phantom' image.

So, what were the results of the royal jelly trials using Kirlian photography? They are clear enough from the photographs in the colour plate section. Two series of photographs were taken on two separate occasions. In the first series of photographs, taken with a three-second exposure, a capsule of the most potent variety of fresh royal jelly showed emissions similar to those given off by a living animal, while the other two capsules — one of royal jelly claiming to be 'fresh' but preserved with vegetable oil rather than honey and wheatgerm oil, and the other a freeze-dried product — revealed hardly any emissions at all. During this session, samples of royal jelly tonic, of royal jelly and honey spread, and of royal jelly and Vitamin E cream were photographed. The royal jelly tonic, in particular, gave startling results. The photograph showed what researchers describe as a 'globule effect', indicating an additional life force over and above what would be considered normal. When this is seen in Kirlian photographs of people, it indicates extra vitality.

The second photography session used longer, six-second exposures for each shot in order to reveal increased illumination of the 'life flux lines'. This session produced even more amazing results.

As before, the freeze-dried capsule revealed no detectable 'life force' although this time the cheap 'fresh' royal jelly capsule did show some signs of life. However, the most potent fresh royal jelly capsule showed very distinct life force fields, and its well-balanced emissions proved the lack of impurities in the capsule. Both royal jelly with honey and royal jelly tonic showed characteristics which indicated that they would be absorbed very quickly into the body to give fast-acting results.

As in the first session, royal jelly and vitamin E cream produced emissions which covered the whole spectrum of energy, but this time, two extra tests were included. A photograph was taken of a finger tip. Subsequently, the finger was massaged with royal jelly and vitamin E cream, then wiped clean with a sterilized cloth and, after five minutes, the finger was photographed again. The difference was remarkable, as the photographs in the colour plate section show.

So, two important inferences can be drawn from these Kirlian photography tests. The first is that high-quality fresh royal jelly products are a much more powerful energy source than cheaper 'fresh' varieties. The second inference to be drawn is that there is absolutely no comparison between the potency of high-quality fresh royal jelly and the almost inert freeze-dried product.

Subsequently, the radiation field of a subject after taking fresh royal jelly tonic was tested. The results are shown in the chart (see Fig 13) and trace the path of the blue and red frequencies over time. The significance of blue or red frequencies may escape the layman, but it is believed that red frequencies represent energy, the 'vital force', nervous and glandular activity — in short, all forms of vitality and power. As can be seen from the chart, the red frequencies increased within the first half hour, peaking after an hour and a half.

As for the blue frequencies, these tend to 'balance' the red, without detracting from the latter's power. So it is that blue represents a calming effect, an increase in intuitive awareness, contentment and tranquillity of mind. The chart shows that the

Royal Jelly Tonic

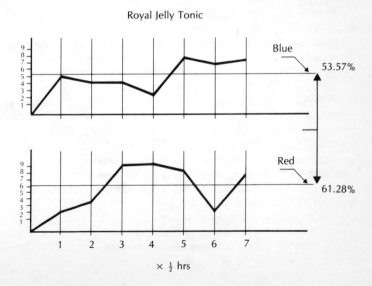

Fig 13 Radiation field chart

subject's blue frequencies increased quite steadily during the three-and-a-half-hour test, and that they were still increasing at the end of that time.

In fact, this test reflects accurately the sensations experienced by anyone who uses fresh royal jelly tonic, a very fast boost of energy and mental powers, increasing and being maintained over a considerable period of time.

———— Latest developments ————

Shortly before finishing this book, I received the results of a series of trials carried out by Harry Oldfield. They made such absorbing reading that I decided to summarize the findings and set them down here.

Mr Oldfield could be described as an 'alternative practitioner and researcher' since, as well as treating a variety of patients, he is also pushing back the frontiers of medical knowledge and treatments with his innovative experimental research. He was an early pioneer of Kirlian photography in Britain and is now the Founder-Principal of the International School of Electrocrystal Therapy.

Harry made use of electrocrystal therapy in one of his fresh royal jelly trials. This therapy involves sending square-pulsed electromagnetic waves through crystals. The crystals vibrate at varying frequencies and Harry first discovers the one which produces a frequency that evokes a sympathetic resonance in the patient's body. The treatment restores those areas of the body which are resonating abnormally and therefore denoting an unhealthy condition.

For this initial trial, which he describes as a 'Pilot Study' since there was no control group or double-blind element to underpin the results, Harry treated patients with cancer, multiple sclerosis, arthritis and ME, as well as a group of people suffering from various conditions. In addition to the electrocrystal therapy, he gave each patient a month's supply of fresh royal jelly capsules. The ME and MS sufferers also received a supply of liquid royal jelly tonic.

At the end of the month, all the patients reported increased energy levels and improvement in their conditions. Arthritis was the only condition which did not seem to respond, but this does not surprise me since it can take up to three months for the symptoms of arthritis to be eased by royal jelly. Harry concluded that 'the circumstantial evidence for using royal jelly in cases of severe illness is very strong indeed, and we have also concluded that the product seems free of side-effects. We therefore have no hesitation in recommending such supplements to other researchers in this field.'

Harry also compared the performances of various fresh royal jelly products, freeze-dried royal jelly and a control solution in prolonging the life of human cells. The reason he elected to run this test was that he wanted to rule out the subjective response which is always present when such tests involve people.

The cells were scraped painlessly from the mouths of volunteers, then transferred to the various culture media solutions, made up using the various royal jelly products. The results were as I expected!

The cells in the control solution lived only three to six hours before showing signs of degeneration and bacterial attack.

Those in the fresh royal jelly capsule solution survived several days before showing signs of deterioration.

Fresh royal jelly tonic gave the most remarkable results. Two weeks after the beginning of the tests the cells showed no sign of deterioration. What is more, Harry discovered in a subsequent test that cells placed in a solution of this tonic could be frozen and thawed with no ill effects.

Lastly, most of the cell lines placed in the solution of freeze-dried royal jelly did not survive as long as they did in the fresh culture and they did not have the same type of protection against bacterial attack.

Yet again, my conviction that fresh royal jelly is more potent than the freeze-dried variety has been confirmed scientifically!

However, Harry had one more test result which added even greater weight to my conviction. He used computerized spectral analysis to examine the energy waveforms of various products, including fresh royal jelly capsules, fresh royal jelly tonic, fresh royal jelly and honey, and freeze-dried royal jelly. Before you look at the computer print-outs illustrated below, I should explain that the more 'disturbed' the surface and profile of the diagram, the more energy and power the product contains.

As you can see, the control product (common salt), produced a virtually flat result, and freeze-dried royal jelly performed little better. However, once you move to the fresh royal jelly products, the immense energy they contain is immediately visible. As with Kirlian photography, the liquid royal jelly tonic gave the most astonishing result.

Indeed, the fascinating aspect of both Harry Oldfield's tests and the Kirlian photography trial is that the results were consistent throughout. In all of them, fresh royal jelly proved markedly superior to the freeze-dried alternative. Of course, I have believed this for many years, but it is always reassuring to have one's beliefs confirmed by hard, scientific facts!

Royal Jelly

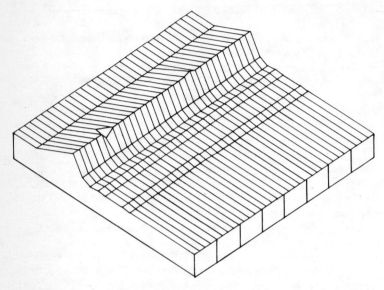

Fig 14a Control product – common salt

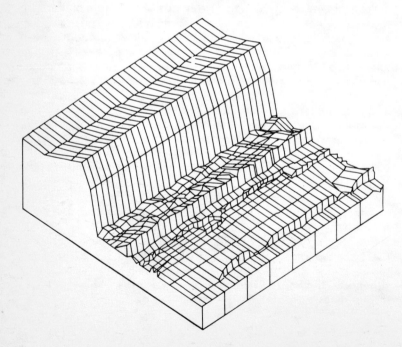

Fig 14b Freeze-dried royal jelly capsule

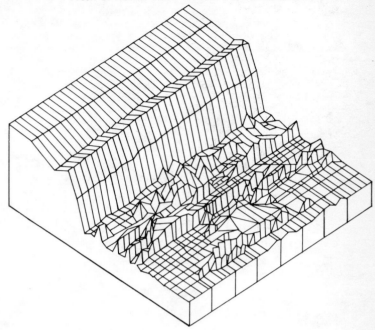

Fig 14c Fresh capsule

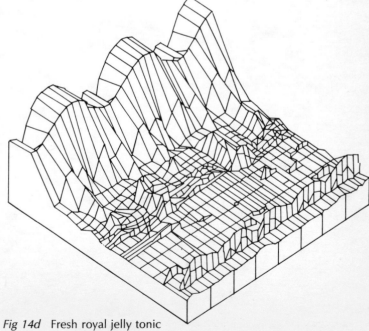

Fig 14d Fresh royal jelly tonic

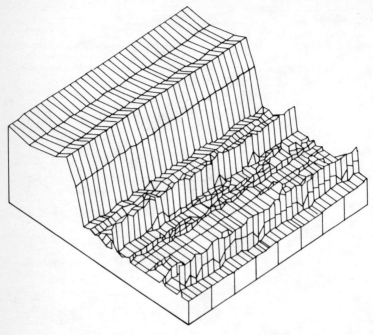

Fig 14e Royal jelly and honey

CHAPTER 6

Royal jelly — the rising star

———Spreading through the world———

There are few countries where royal jelly has failed to make an impact as a key agent in promoting good health. Certainly, the honey bee has spread a long way from its prehistoric homeland somewhere in the depths of Asia: by the time bees were imported to New Zealand in 1842 they were already established on all the major land masses of the world.

Sadly, it took much longer for the food news about royal jelly to spread from Asia to the West. However, now that it has, the royal jelly market is mushrooming with more and more people in different lands realizing the benefits of this precious substance.

Royal jelly has been firmly established in France for many years now, so much so that it even used to be sold by the side of the road! Further east, the Arab world has long thought of 'bee milk' as an aphrodisiac and the popularity of royal jelly in those countries continues to rise.

British royal jelly products are now exported to more than 40 countries, including the EEC countries, Hong Kong, Singapore and, of course, the health-conscious United States of America. What is more, there is a distinct possibility of Britain 'taking coals to Newcastle', since the Chinese the major producers of fresh royal jelly, are interested in importing these British products which contain Chinese royal jelly!

More countries throughout the world are now beginning to produce royal jelly to meet the increasing demand. Although the Chinese variety is still the best, beekeepers in other areas are doing their best to match up to the high standards and quantity of royal jelly production in China. Mexico, for example, has a long tradition of beekeeping dating back to the time of the Mayan empire, when the natives used honey and wax for trade, in medicines and for religious ceremonies. Now, however, the beekeepers of the Yuca-tan peninsula have recognized the need to diversify and are developing the production of royal jelly with a vengeance.

The Taiwanese, in contrast, are relative newcomers to the beekeeping world. They have moved into the production of honey, beeswax and royal jelly because this activity generates a much higher income than the traditional rice crop. Japan is Taiwan's principal export market for royal jelly, with the last 7 years seeing a rapid increase in demand.

Interestingly, a questionnaire was given to Japanese royal jelly consumers and as many as 80 per cent reported beneficial effects from using the product. This success rate is very impressive when the difficulties in assessing the benefits of royal jelly are considered; the effects are felt slowly, taking several months to become fully apparent.

As one might expect, more and more benefits of fresh royal jelly are becoming known and reports I have received from overseas have started to sound very familiar. A lady from New York State says,

> My youngest son, Joseph, has always been on the sickly side, with frequent colds, pale complexion, underweight and just in general not as mentally alert as he should be.
>
> Joseph has been on royal jelly for the past six weeks. He is doing so well now. His appetite has greatly increased and he has gained about seven pounds. He has much more color in his face... Mentally, it has done wonders as he is happier and more alert.

A Malaysian royal jelly enthusiast reports,

> Before starting on the royal jelly capsules I was having irregular periods, hormone imbalance, hair loss and a weight problem. At the same time I had severe backache, abdomen discomfort and poor circulation in my feet every morning for more than two years after the birth of my first child. I was so happy and surprised that within a month after taking the royal jelly capsules, all my ailments had disappeared, and furthermore after three months my hair started to grow in abundance and is now much healthier. I have also lost about 12 lb in weight.

And so it goes on. A Greek lady who had suffered with acne for 11 years found that the condition improved after only three months, while a gentleman in Germany says that, after one year on the capsules, 'my overall health has improved 100 per cent'.

Why has the royal jelly way of life spread so rapidly around the world? I believe it must have something to do with the increased speed of communications in the last two decades. With so many people travelling to far-flung holiday spots and the instant impact of today's sophisticated media, news — even the good variety — travels faster than ever before.

Added to this is the increased interest worldwide in Eastern traditions and beliefs. With this has come an interest in Eastern medicine, particularly acupuncture. Many people were initially very sceptical about the value of this technique, which uses needles inserted in specific points of the body to relieve pain and assist healing. More recently it has become very popular, simply because it works! There is in fact a scientific basis for the success of acupuncture treatment since it is now known that the needles stimulate production of endorphins, the body's own painkillers.

A similar process is occurring with royal jelly; the good news spread by word of mouth and through the media is snowballing. It will not be long before research is carried out in the West which will convince the scientific community once and for all that it works!

The story of royal jelly's phenomenal success in the United States is an absorbing one and involves a remarkable lady named Madeline Balletta.

Back in 1981 Madeline developed an illness thought by her doctors to be multiple sclerosis (since diagnosed as chronic Epstein-Barr virus). A concerned friend introduced Madeline to the top British brand of fresh royal jelly and the results were amazing. Since then Madeline has praised God daily for His gift of royal jelly.

After Madeline had been taking the capsules for many months her condition had improved so markedly that the doctors believed the disease was in remission. Madeline decided to stop taking royal jelly and gradually all the symptoms reappeared. When she resumed her daily regime, the improvement was dramatic. Madeline says, 'I believe that royal jelly builds up my immune system and helps my body to fight back. I know I'm not cured, but I'm able to lead a very normal and active life.'

Madeline's son Jason, who suffered from bronchial asthma, was next to experience the remarkable benefits of royal jelly. At this point, Madeline realized that this wonderful substance could be of help to people suffering from varying conditions, and she began to hand it out to relatives and friends. The results were more than impressive — they astonished her.

Madeline then decided to set up a distribution company so that all of America could have access to the myriad benefits of royal jelly. Today this company is becoming known throughout America: big oaks from little acorns grow!

—————— Spreading through society ——————

Added impetus has been given to royal jelly's progress by the news that some of the most influential people in modern society are fervent believers in its powers. For instance, Margaret Thatcher, the British Prime Minister, recently revealed that she was interested in its effects on jet lag.

Moving even higher in society, few people can have failed to read that Their Royal Highnesses the Princess of Wales and the Duchess of York took fresh royal jelly during their pregnancies. It was even claimed that both the Duchess and the Duke of York turned to the liquid tonic as a means of boosting their chances of having a baby. There have also been reports that Prince Charles, who is of course a great believer in natural medicine, follows the royal jelly regime and that both Her Majesty the queen and the Duke of Edinburgh take it regularly, too.

Another royal family which swears by the benefits of fresh royal jelly is that of the principality of Monaco. Her Serene Highness the Princess Antoinette of Monaco says,

> My daughters, grandchildren as well as myself are delighted with royal jelly products. We find they provide energy and help one to keep off colds, 'flu, etc.
> When I have a very heavy day ahead, a dose of liquid royal jelly tonic really helps me to get through it successfully.

—————— Spreading through the stars ——————

The men and women involved in show business are no more immune to the stresses, strains and niggling ailments of everyday life than any other section of the population. In fact, many of them lead more stressed lives than the average person, having to cope with action-packed spells interspersed with periods of relative leisure.

Given this variable pattern of energy requirements, many of today's stars find fresh royal jelly capsules and tonic invaluable in their careers. Among the stars of popular music who enjoy the benefits of fresh royal jelly are Cliff Richard, Pat Boone, Lulu, Joe Brown and Kim Wilde. Cliff and Joe in particular are long-time royal jelly fans, and this shows not only in their enviable energy but also in their youthful appearance. Even Cliff himself wonders at his amazing energy: 'I play tennis daily: concerts I breeze through and recording sessions are a doddle. Could it be the royal jelly?'

An alternative practitioner recommended fresh royal jelly to Joe Brown about twelve years ago, when the pop singer's health and nervous state were at a low ebb. 'It really does perk me up — I'd be lost without it', says Joe. 'I recommended it to all my mates, including Dora Bryan, and my wife, Vicky, takes it, too.' As well as giving him the energy to cope with a demanding work schedule, royal jelly also seems to keep Joe's weight stable. A keen supporter of natural medicines, Joe adds, 'It's a pity so many people resort to pep pills and drugs when there are natural products like royal jelly which can bring good health, a sense of well-being and the ability to cope with everyday problems.'

In the United States of America, a recent convert to royal jelly is Pat Boone. The singer is so impressed with the improvement in his health and energy levels since taking royal jelly that he has encouraged listeners to his weekly rock gospel radio programme to try the capsules themselves. This is 'spreading the word' with a vengeance!

Some of today's most energetic actors and actresses also find that royal jelly gives them extra reserves of stamina when they would otherwise be asleep on their feet. Karl Howman, best known as Jacko from the BBC television series 'Brush Strokes', was recently working an 18-hour day, seven days a week, not only in the television studios but also on the London stage in nightly performances of 'Me and My Girl'. He is convinced that it was liquid royal jelly tonic which enabled him to survive this punishing schedule.

Two other comedy stars who maintain equally hectic schedules thanks to royal jelly are the superb actresses Maureen Lipman and Lysette Anthony. Lysette is familiar to television viewers from the BBC series 'Three Up, Two Down', and her days are a cocktail of television commercials, regular commuting between Paris and London, a busy keep-fit programme and her 'day job' as an actress! 'Over the last year,' Lysette told me recently, 'I've hardly had a day off, and some days can be one hell of a haul, I can tell you! I'm not sure that I'd ever keep going without my daily royal jelly capsules.' She found other pluses from taking the capsules: 'As part of a balanced diet, royal jelly really helps me to maintain a good complexion, and for the first time I've been able to grow long, healthy fingernails.'

Talking of keeping fit, even the healthiest of us needs a little help to keep in top form, as Lizzy Webb — the breakfast television fitness and beauty expert — knows only too well. Lizzy, of course, is in superb physical shape, but royal jelly still has its part to play in her life. 'Since taking royal jelly capsules, I have noticed a marked difference in my skin. Even at the very early stages of taking just one capsule every morning, make-up ladies at work noticed a "glowing smoothness", so its effects were obviously quick to show.'

Television personality Jan Leeming has been taking royal jelly capsules ever since she met me two years ago. Jan recently told me,

Since that time I have had far fewer colds than ever before. I had been plagued with colds and sore throats most of my life which are definitely not conducive to the work of a broadcaster. I have just finished five weeks in pantomime and during the run many of the cast went down with colds and 'flu. I am delighted to say that I managed to avoid both.

Jan is sensibly sparing in her use of royal jelly tonic, but says, 'on the rare occasions that I use it I definitely find it gives me an energy boost'.

Katie Boyle is another personality who would not be without her regular daily dose of royal jelly. She is particularly enthusiastic about the liquid tonic. Katie may have given up some of her regular commitments, but her life is nevertheless action-packed. 'Even though I'm still working flat out, I can keep going much more. That's not to say I don't get exhausted, because I do. But the thought of a hectic day doesn't horrify me any more. And what is more, the tonic doesn't stop me sleeping, which is very important.'

Among other women celebrities who find that royal jelly helps them to keep healthy and cope with an extra busy life are the romantic novelist Barbara Cartland and Gloria Hunniford, star of radio and television.

———— Spreading through the sports world ————

Another area where royal jelly is gaining a reputation is in the sports world. Athletes may be at the peak of fitness, but that does not mean that their energy supplies are inexhaustible. I understand that Jimmy Savile's remarkable tally of 169 marathons was helped along by royal jelly, and he is not the only marathon runner who finds it invaluable. Fraser Clyne travels all over the world, for example to Australia, the United States and Japan, to take part in long-distance races. When Fraser's wife first suggested that he take royal jelly to help him in his running, he was very sceptical.

'Just another health food gimmick', I thought. But I was willing to try anything which might sustain my 100 miles per week training schedule. After a few months of taking one royal jelly capsule on a daily basis my initial scepticism began to wane. I noticed a definite improvement in my general well-being. I didn't feel nearly as tired as usual... in full training I usually felt permanently fatigued, but that all began to change. The longer I went with royal jelly, the more convinced I became of its benefits, not only for people who run 100 miles per week, but for all runners, joggers and indeed anyone interested in maintaining an active lifestyle. Throughout the winter months

I was subject to fewer colds and infections than ever before, and on the rare occasions when I did pick up a virus I seemed to shrug it off far more quickly than in the past.

A keen runner in Germany reported similar benefits.

In my training I run about 80 miles a week and marathons, etc, and have trained throughout last winter 15°C below freezing, (5°F), in rain, snow, ice, etc. Since I have been taking royal jelly capsules I have never had a cold or 'flu, and my general training has vastly improved.

A Cheshire athlete was not up to the standard of either of these two old hands (or, come to that, of Sebastian Coe, another runner who made royal jelly part of his training schedule), but even she found that royal jelly could make the running easy.

Last year I foolishly (ambitiously) entered a 40-mile challenge run. I expected to walk most of it, and I hoped to finish within the 15 hours allowed.

Whilst packing the plasters and spare socks, I came across two phials of royal jelly tonic. I took one an hour before setting off, and the other at about 28 miles. I romped round and finished in 8 hours 10 mins! I felt superbly confident throughout the run.

Of course, athletics is just one of the sports where increased stamina, sustained concentration and peak fitness are essential. Two women sporting stars from the worlds of cricket and three-day eventing who rely on royal jelly are ex-captain of England Rachel Heyhoe-Flint and Lucinda Green. I think their achievement of excellence speaks for itself!

There are other areas of sporting endeavour where success is not a target but essential. One such is that of professional football: if you cannot produce the results you may find yourself out of a job! Several football teams from all divisions of the Football League have used royal jelly to boost their stamina, including Aston Villa, Glasgow Rangers, Norwich, Queens Park Rangers, Oxford and Millwall FC, who raced up the league once they started on a royal jelly regime. Their fortunes improved steadily on their bee-milk diet to the extent that they were promoted to the First Division for the first time in 109 years!

The recipe for Millwall's success included a daily capsule of fresh royal jelly plus a phial of tonic before each match. Not only did this regime help them to many impressive victories, but it also speeded recovery from any injuries the players were unlucky enough to sustain. Frank McLintock, Assistant Manager of the club at the time of writing, was already a honey fanatic when he came across royal jelly and is now one of its most enthusiastic supporters: 'It gives me a feeling of well-being and I shall continue to use it in the future.'

A Second Division professional footballer also adheres to the Millwall royal jelly diet. He says, 'I find the liquid tonic, in particular, is useful taken just before a game, helping me to compete to maximum potential for the whole of the game.'

As you will notice, there are consistent threads in these opinions on royal jelly: boosted energy; improved skin, nails and hair; resistance to viral infections: and increased well-being. All of these — except perhaps for improved skin, nails and hair — *could* be dismissed as being potentially psychological in origin, but there are many instances and scientific proof of the quite astonishing results which royal jelly can have on specific diseases and ailments. If you are in relatively good health when you begin taking royal jelly, it could be hard for you to decide whether it is the royal jelly which is making you feel so much better, or simply the psychological effect of taking it. As I have already said, it does not really matter that much, but in cases where the mind can have only limited power over a painful or debilitating physical condition, the fact that royal jelly really does work is vitally important. I shall be looking at some of these conditions in the next chapter.

CHAPTER 7

The natural medicine chest

In this chapter I shall concentrate mainly on royal jelly as a treatment during times of illness, but we must not lose sight of its many benefits when taken by healthy people. It can give us extra energy, thick lustrous hair, beautiful skin, strong nails, resistance to infection, and an undefinable glow of well-being. Then, in the unlikely event that we fall ill despite taking a regular course of royal jelly, it puts us back on the road to recovery, even when conventional medicine can do nothing to help. On top of that, it has no known side-effects (except good ones!).

The ordinary user of royal jelly products may find it hard to envisage going to consult a GP and coming away with a prescription for royal jelly capsules, cream or liquid tonic. How much more difficult, then, must it be to contemplate a hospital where the only medicines used were products of the hive, where injections of royal jelly were a routine treatment!

There is one country, however, where this does occur and, as you will have realized by now, that country is China. I have already made some mention of the Apitherapy Hospital at Lianyungang, where a great deal of the medical research on bee products is carried out and where, indeed, these products are the only medicines used to treat a variety of ailments.

The standard dose of royal jelly at the Apitherapy Hospital, according to Professor Fang Zhu, its Research Director, is 0.5 mg of the fresh substance which is used as it is, or mixed with honey, then placed under the patient's tongue for fast absorption into the system. The treatment is used to boost energy and the immune system, thereby increasing resistance to disease. 20 years ago the Chinese began to inject patients with royal jelly, and this technique is still used for people suffering from arthritis and hepatitis, as well as those who have trouble sleeping.

I was surprised, nevertheless, at the limited range of diseases for which royal jelly is a standard Chinese treatment, since over the many years of my interest in the subject, I have come across a remarkably wide spread of ailments which respond to royal jelly. Even ME (myalgic encephalitis), a condition which has only recently been identified, seems to respond, and several ailments which improve after royal jelly treatment when they occur in humans will also improve when they appear in animals.

—————————— In sickness ... ——————————

Acne

Adolescence is the time of life which we usually associate with acne, but some unfortunate people have to deal with it well into adulthood. Teenagers are told to avoid fatty foods as this can help to keep the pores clear, but this is a period when hormones are swinging wildly and there is plenty of grease being exuded through the pores, clogging them, becoming infected and resulting in the dreaded spots. Happily, whatever your age, if you suffer from this distressing condition royal jelly is full of ingredients which will clear the problem — sulphur, phosphorus, biotin, vitamin C and the B vitamins all have a part to play. Consequently, it is advisable for acne sufferers to embark on a royal jelly capsule regime both as a treatment and as a preventive measure. It is also well known that vitamin E applied externally to skin eruptions proves very beneficial, so applying royal jelly cream with vitamin E should deal the condition a mortal blow.

AIDS

Acquired Immune Deficiency Syndrome is a terrible disease which is affecting an increasingly wide cross-section of humanity and for which, at the time of writing, there is no known cure. However, the ability of royal jelly to boost the immune system and improve overall health would be invaluable to those who have been diagnosed HIV-positive, and even to those who have gone on to develop AIDS itself.

Allergies

There are almost as many manifestations of allergies as there are allergens: headaches, hay fever, stomach upsets, asthma, skin rashes, swellings, etc. The sensible course is to keep well away from the allergens once these have been identified, but this is sometimes easier said than done. It is very difficult, for example, to avoid pollen or to be sure that nothing one eats in a restaurant contains eggs or gluten.

In addition, many of orthodox medicine's treatments are worryingly strong (steroid creams immediately spring to mind), and it is well worth trying a course of royal jelly to see whether it can help. I have already cited the case of the gentleman who found that he no longer had to suffer the annual misery of hay fever after taking royal jelly for an extended period. There are many ingredients in this substance which might be responsible for his relief, but the most likely candidate is glutamic acid, one of the amino acids.

Anaemia

Anaemia literally means 'lack of blood', but it actually describes a condition in which the amount of oxygen-carrying red haemoglobin in the blood is insufficient. The result is uncharacteristic tiredness, shortness of breath and pallor. There can be few more effective treatments for anaemia which are free of side-effects than royal jelly. It contains the mineral and the vitamins essential to haemoglobin production — iron, plus vitamin B12 and folic acid. It has the added bonus of hydroxydecanoic acid with its blood-conditioning properties.

Anaemia can often be so mild that it goes unnoticed, especially in women who have heavy periods and thus have difficulty in manufacturing enough haemoglobin to maintain the proper levels. This may be behind some of the cases of women who report especially significant increases in energy after taking royal jelly. They may have become tired and listless due to mild anaemia.

Angina

The chest pains of angina are extremely frightening and often indicate constriction of the coronary arteries due to arteriosclerosis (see below). However, this pain can also be caused by a deficient oxygen supply to the heart muscle because there is not enough haemoglobin (the red oxygen-carrying pigment) in the blood. It is known that royal jelly increases haemoglobin levels, as explained under Anaemia. Consequently, many angina sufferers find relief after a course of royal jelly capsules.

Anorexia nervosa

To call this the 'slimmer's disease' is to inaccurately define and make light of a life-threatening affliction. Often, anorexia is the result of a psychological disturbance, either the reluctance of a pubescent girl to come to terms with the implications either of adulthood or her own sexuality, or an expression of very low self-esteem or even self-hate. There have recently been suggestions that even this psychological disturbance is dietetic in origin, caused by a mineral deficiency.

Although royal jelly cannot cure this dreadful disease, it can at

least act as a valuable dietary supplement since it is such a rich
cocktail of vitamins, minerals and amino acids. It can also help to
lift associated depression and minimize stress, all of which may
provide a breathing space in the relentless downhill slide of the
anorexic.

Arteriosclerosis

This is the medical name for any condition in which the walls of
the arteries become hard, thick and therefore narrower than they
should be. Frequently, arteriosclerosis manifests itself as atherosclerosis, in which fatty deposits build up inside the arteries,
creating ideal conditions for a blood clot or thrombosis to form
with the concomitant risk of a heart attack or stroke. The obvious
way to avoid such a build-up is to cut down on the consumption of
animal fats. However, some people's bodies seem to have difficulty in metabolizing even small amounts of fat and they have high
cholesterol levels in their blood. In such cases, or if someone is
eating a diet which is relatively high in fat, it would be advisable to
take royal jelly, since the inositol it contains contributes to the
manufacture within the body of lecithin, the fat and cholesterol
metabolizer *par excellence.*

That royal jelly actually controls blood cholesterol levels has
been shown in several experiments. One such experiment was carried out by some Japanese scientists in the Hoshi College of Phar-
macy. They found that royal jelly had very little effect on the blood
cholesterol of rabbits where this was normal but that, when
another group of rabbits was fed a high-cholesterol diet together
with royal jelly, the cholesterol level in their blood was lower than
that in rabbits fed a cholesterol-rich diet without the royal jelly.
This points yet again to the 'normalizing' function of this amazing
substance. Where the cholesterol level was satisfactory, royal jelly
was virtually ineffective, whereas where the cholesterol level
would normally have been high, royal jelly lowered it. (An Argenti-
nian experiment carried this one step further and demonstrated
that royal jelly could even remove induced fatty deposits in rabbits'
arteries.)

Where human patients are concerned, a report from St Mary's
Hospital, Brooklyn, New York, states that three patients, with different case histories, but all with high cholesterol and/or
triglyceride levels, were given one teaspoonful of royal jelly twice
daily and that after two weeks levels of both were lower.

Arthritis

Arthritis is one of the conditions where treatment with royal jelly
has been the subject of intensive scientific and medical research. I

have already mentioned that the Chinese give routine injections of royal jelly to cure arthritis, but published research has been carried out in England, too.

In the 1960s, Dr Barton-Wright, a biochemist, and W.A. Elliott, Physician-in-charge of the Rheumatic Clinic at St Alfege's Hospital London, investigated the pantothenic acid levels in four groups of people. The first group were meat-eaters who did not suffer from arthritis, the second arthritis-free vegetarians, the third rheumatoid arthritics on a normal balanced diet, and the fourth arthritic vegetarians. The scientists found that the mean pantothenic acid levels were by far the highest in the non-arthritic vegetarians, followed by the non-arthritic meat eaters, with both groups of rheumatoid arthritics coming in a poor joint third.

The two scientists tried giving intramuscular injections of pantothenic acid in the form of calcium-d-pantothenate to the two arthritic groups, with some success. However, although the level of pantothenic acid in their blood rose to that of the meat-eating non-arthritics, it would not rise any higher, despite continued injections, and began to fall back to its previous level once treatment had been discontinued, with ensuing reappearance of the symptoms.

It was obvious that the arthritics had some problem in retaining pantothenic acid, so the two men looked around for a solution and decided to try injections of royal jelly since this substance is the richest natural source of available pantothenic acid. They had read of Townsend et al's success in completely protecting mice against transplantable leukaemia using hydroxydecanoic acid and, since royal jelly is the only known natural source of this fatty acid, they felt that the combination of both acids might have a more potent and lasting effect. They were right! Combined royal jelly and pantothenic acid injections raised the blood pantothenic acid of both vegetarian and non-vegetarian arthritics to much higher levels than were possible with pantothenic acid alone (up to sixty per cent higher in some of the vegetarian arthritics) with rapid relief of arthritic symptoms over 28 days in the case of the non-vegetarians, and complete disappearance of the symptoms within 14 days in the case of the vegetarians.

The response with vegetarians was markedly superior. Of the ten patients treated daily over a 15-month period, only one showed any sign of the symptoms returning, and that sign was only slight. Since daily injections proved inconvenient and uncomfortable, it was fortunate that oral treatment looked likely to be equally effective.

The message is clear. If you have arthritis, you would be well advised to switch to a vegetarian diet (or at least cut out red meat) and take royal jelly daily. For faster relief, you could try taking a vitamin B5 (pantothenic acid) supplement as well.

I have evidence in my own family of the value of royal jelly in treating arthritis, for my mother was once virtually crippled by the disease. However, now, at almost 80 years of age and after many years on a royal jelly regime, she is completely free of pain and has excellent mobility.

Asthma

An attack of asthma can be brought on by many different stimuli — bronchitis, stress, or reaction to an allergen. We have already seen that royal jelly can be helpful in relieving allergies, and it also has several ingredients which reduce stress and will fight infection, wherever in the body it may be.

Back pain

Sciatica, lumbago, slipped discs — all of these account for a large proportion of days off work in all manner of occupations. It is one of the unaccountable effects of royal jelly that it can relieve a wide range of pain of diverse origin. Perhaps this is because it attacks on various fronts: through oxygenating the blood and thereby speeding healing of torn muscles or ligaments; relaxing tense muscles and reducing stress; fighting infection and inflammation; combating arthritis; and relieving fatigue. Then again, the analgesia may be part of the synergetic effect of royal jelly. Whatever the case, I hear of many people who have experienced relief from back pain with royal jelly. Mrs V. from Derby wrote,

> I had been suffering from sciatica and lumbago for many years; in fact I'd forgotten what it was like to feel free of pain until I decided to try royal jelly capsules. I've never looked back. My aches and pains grew less and less as the weeks went on, until now, after six months of taking it I feel a different person.

Bronchitis

Acute bronchitis often follows a cold or a bout of influenza when the body is already weakened by viral infection, leaving it open to bacterial infection, too. Royal jelly, with the antibiotic properties of hydroxydecanoic acid, can help to clear up the bronchitis, or even prevent it from developing in the first place. Many people find that they develop increased resistance to colds and 'flu when taking royal jelly and that, if they do catch either, it is very shortlived, relatively mild and clears up without complications.

Cancer

Royal jelly can benefit cancer sufferers by boosting the body's resistance to the harmful side-effects of chemotherapy and radiotherapy both before and after treatment. Indeed, Professor Fang Zhu at the Apitherapy Hospital in China believes that royal jelly could give some protection against cancer by improving the immune system. There are certainly ingredients in royal jelly which could give one cause to believe that there is a scientific basis for any helpful effects experienced by cancer sufferers. To begin with, hydroxydecanoic acid — the fatty acid unique to royal jelly — has been shown to inhibit transplantable leukaemia in mice, and the trace mineral cobalt is used in modern cancer-bombarding drugs, while glutamic acid helps the body to withstand chemotherapy and radiotherapy. That being said, one could not say with certainty that these substances are present in sufficient quantities to have a therapeutic effect, and even if they were, one could not be sure that the results would be predictable, given that the substances work in harness in royal jelly and not autonomously.

However, I have received several reports from America from cancer patients describing very positive results from using royal jelly. One lady from New York State recommends royal jelly highly to other cancer patients and has a remarkable story to tell.

> I was diagnosed as having breast cancer in December of '82. Both breasts were affected, and it had already begun to spread to three ribs. The treatment involved removal of the ovaries, bilateral mastectomy, and massive doses of chemotherapy for eight consecutive weeks and thereafter every other week indefinitely.
>
> While I did not experience severe side-effects of chemotherapy, I did have minor discomforts throughout these three and a half years. I would get mouth sores, cramps in my legs, feet and hands, lingering colds and fatigue. By May '86 I was run down from a cold that I had for five and a half months, and all the other discomforts were increasing. I was tired of feeling sick all the time.
>
> With my doctor's permission, I began taking royal jelly. In one week my cold was gone. After one month I was able to stay awake for an entire day and function normally. The cramps were almost completely gone, and the mouth sores were responding to medication. I wanted to be sure that royal jelly was the factor that improved my condition so I finished my three months supply and did not renew it for two months. All of the symptoms returned and I again began to feel tired all the time.

Another lady from Pearl River was fortunate enough to know about royal jelly before she began months of chemotherapy treatment following a partial mastectomy.

> My doctor told me my energy level would be affected. I would undoubtedly lose my hair and develop sores in my mouth. Because of these things, I decided to take one phial of royal jelly tonic and two capsules before each treatment. I would like to say by the end of my treatments of chemotherapy, I had very little loss of hair, no sores in my mouth *and* surprisingly good energy and emotionally fared very well.

Cold sores

Herpes simplex is a virus which results in the common cold sore, an unsightly and annoying condition which can sometimes persist for weeks. The virus is frequently present in the mouths of healthy carriers and is spread by personal contact. Royal jelly's healing and skin-improving ingredients soon clear up the lesion, while the many energizing and health-giving elements boost the immune system and can provide resistance to infection. It may be also that pyridoxine encourages the production of antibodies, preventing further attacks.

I am beginning to wonder whether something in royal jelly has a widespread anti-viral action, given the frequently reported increase in resistance to a multitude of infections from the common cold to childhood diseases, and the speedy recovery which many royal jelly users experience from any viral infections they do contract (*see*, for example, Glandular fever and Hepatitis).

Cystitis

Although cystitis can affect both men and women, it is more common in women because of the shortness of the female urethra, which enables bacteria to reach the bladder more easily. There are many self-help methods for avoiding or alleviating attacks of this unpleasant complaint, but the disappearance of intractable cystitis is often a beneficial side-effect of taking royal jelly capsules, due to the bactericidal action of hydroxydecanoic acid and the resistance to infection which pantothenic acid provides.

Depression

It is often difficult to differentiate between depression and an anxiety state, since the two can manifest themselves in a similar way. This is why someone might go to his or her GP complaining that he or she is very depressed only to be given tranquillizers. Both tranquillizers and anti-depressants are very powerful drugs with very troubling side-effects, including addiction where some tranquillizers are concerned (see below). Happily, royal jelly has a host of ingredients which can help to lift depression: thiamine, glutamic acid, phenylalanine, tyrosine, iron and riboflavin. One of the results almost always reported by users of royal jelly is a lifting of spirits together with a feeling of increased well-being. This applies whether the subject is suffering from anxiety or depression and is a further instance of royal jelly's 'normalizing' effect on the whole body.

Dermatitis

There are so many helpful ingredients in royal jelly where skin rashes are concerned, such as pantothenic acid, sulphur, phosphorus, biotin, niacin and riboflavin, that it is not surprising that dermatitis responds readily to this substance whether it is taken internally or applied externally. Of course, in 'contact dermatitis' the inflammation is a response to an external irritant, so it is wise to identify that irritant (often wool or biological washing powders) since prevention is always better than cure! The rash may also be the result of an allergy to a particular food item and this should be investigated if no external irritant can be found. Since royal jelly seems to reduce allergic responses, perhaps because of its glutamic acid content, there should be some relief, even if the nature of the allergen remains a mystery.

Disability

When a child is born mentally disabled, the general reaction is to sympathize with both the parents and the child, but to assume that nothing much can be done to help. Magda Ryman, founder of Fontis, the Children's Centre for Natural Therapies, has very different ideas. This remarkable lady combines a wide range of complementary treatments, including reflexology, aromatherapy and crystal therapy, with the aim of improving the health and quality of life of her patients.

I first met Magda some four years ago and since that time she has made royal jelly not only a part of her family's daily life, but also an important part of her treatment programme. Magda told me, 'I find royal jelly particularly suitable for any condition where the brain needs nourishing. It is also helpful where there is difficulty in intestinal absorption, especially when vitamin and mineral supplements are not tolerated: this makes it very useful for children with Down's syndrome.'

Magda makes no distinction between different disabilities; she even treats children suffering from the comparatively 'mild' conditions of hyperactivity, asthma and hay fever in her Finchley centre. As far as she is concerned, the main route to improvement is to 'balance the body into an optimum state'. Since a 'balancing' action is one of royal jelly's prime attributes, this valuable natural substance was a clear candidate for the Fontis treatment regime.

At first, Magda gave her patients royal jelly and honey spread, but the children loved it so much that they ate it by the jarful, so now they take their royal jelly in capsule form! Among the results which this dedicated lady has observed in patients taking royal jelly is an increase in energy levels, combined with a calming effect on highly-strung children, in addition to a generalized increase in their powers of concentration.

Magda has found neuro-muscular disorders such as cerebral palsy and Down's syndrome readily responsive to treatment with royal jelly and uses a muscle-testing technique as one way of gauging progress. However, she considers that the most important feedback comes from her patients' parents, as they alone know the children well enough to notice the signs of improvement which even the most observant doctor might miss.

Unfortunately, although muscle testing is recognized as a valid monitoring technique in most countries, it is not recognized by the medical profession in the United Kingdom. Magda's work can be made more difficult by conventional practitioners in other ways too. She told me of one of her patients who had to have an operation to create a fourth chamber in his heart. Unfortunately, he emerged from the anaesthetic with brain damage. A side-effect of this damage is that he is virtually paralysed with fear and has lost his appetite. As an appetite-stimulant, royal jelly would be an ideal treatment for this boy but, sad to say, every time he is readmitted to hospital, the staff will not allow him to continue taking royal jelly, and any progress he has made outside hospital is lost during his stay on the ward.

Since Fontis is a voluntary organization — all the staff give their time completely free of charge — Magda's centre can open only for two afternoons a week. There is no charge for treatment, either: if parents wish, and can afford to, they may make a donation to the centre's funds. It is not surprising that the Children's Centre for Natural Therapies is desperate for funds! Magda would dearly love to open the centre five or six days a week, to purchase better premises to which wheelchair patients may have access, to run some supervised trials and to embark on a proper monitoring programme. I sincerely hope that her fund-raising activities are successful, as I am sure that her work is vital not only to her young patients but also in exploring the possible applications and myriad effects of fresh royal jelly.

Duodenal ulcers

Duodenal ulcers may result from a severe deficiency of pantothenic acid, and since royal jelly is the richest source of this vitamin it could well prevent deterioration of this condition and afford some protection. If ulcers have been induced by stress, royal jelly will act as a natural sedative, thanks to its phosphorus content, while the glutamic acid will soothe irritation.

Dysmenorrhoea (period pains)

Pain is a very subjective sensation in that a dull ache which is tolerable for one person may be torture for another, not because some people are braver than others but because some people are simply more sensitive to pain than others and so have a lower threshold. Period pains do vary in intensity from woman to woman. Some sail through with not even a twinge, while others are in such discomfort that they have to take to their beds each month.

One unfortunate woman who suffered this way was Mrs I. She had had severe dysmenorrhoea for twelve years and had tried every type of analgesic. She had even had a dilation and curettage, but with no success. Then she tried royal jelly capsules and was amazed by the results: 'I don't have to have days off work any more — I don't have to miss anything thanks to royal jelly.'

Royal jelly probably works in two ways in helping to alleviate period pains. Dysmenorrhoea is exacerbated by tension, and it is very difficult to relax when you are in pain, as I am sure we have all found. The natural sedative action of royal jelly therefore helps to reduce the tension, while its analgesic effect relieves the pain.

Eczema

Eczema can be particularly distressing for babies and toddlers as they instinctively scratch the irritating scaly patches and aggravate the condition. Unfortunately, this is a condition which predominantly affects infants, then often disappears as the children approach school age or puberty.

Fortunately, eczema in all age groups responds readily to royal jelly taken internally or applied externally. A Miss Z. from London is one of the many people who have written to me about the effect which royal jelly has had on their eczema. 'Since using royal jelly with vitamin E cream and royal jelly capsules my eczema has completely disappeared, my skin is now free from horrible dry itchy red patches and is now lovely and soft.'

I would always recommend that you use both capsules and cream in tackling eczema. Local applications of the cream will produce excellent results, but the capsules are a systemic remedy, working their way through the body to tackle the problem at its source — whether it be an allergy or the poor circulation which produces varicose eczema.

Fluid retention

When I first took royal jelly, the main complaint which I was hoping to cure was fluid retention. The substance is a natural diuretic and I was delighted with the results. There are various types of fluid retention which lead to swelling of the face, ankles or legs. The three most common causes are kidney malfunction, poor circulation or a thiamine deficiency. Royal jelly contains thiamine to combat the third cause, plenty of ingredients to improve the second and seems to improve kidney function (see Kidney disorders in this chapter).

Gastro-enteritis

Tummy upsets with diarrhoea and vomiting are not too serious in people who are otherwise healthy, but they are very unpleasant and can be life-threatening in babies and the old. Hydroxy-decanoic acid, which occurs only in royal jelly, has been shown to kill two of the most potent bacteria associated with gastro-enteritis, and may well have a bactericidal action on others.

Geriatric disorders

If we are fortunate enough to reach a ripe old age, we can expect to be beset by a variety of health problems, both mental and physical. Royal jelly's ability to improve brain function and mental powers through its glutamic acid, phenylalanine, phosphorus, iron and vitamin B12 content was powerfully demonstrated in a trial with ME sufferers (see Myalgic encephalomyelitis in this chapter), and there are so many of its ingredients which help to boost the immune system, combat infection and relieve many of the distressing ailments which afflict the elderly.

A trial carried out on elderly patients in Loughborough and monitored by a doctor revealed improvements in five areas after a course of royal jelly: increased appetite; weight increase in most patients; mental alertness increased in the majority of the patients; general improvement in hair growth and skin tone; and increased feelings of well-being.

The owner of a home for the elderly in Cardiff monitored the effect of a three-month course of royal jelly on residents and staff with the assistance of a State Registered Nurse. The nurse reported,

Among the elderly residents, a definite improvement was noted in their general health. Considering the trial took place in the winter months, very few illnesses occurred and medical attention was hardly sought.

Glandular fever

Glandular fever is the common name for infectious mono-nucleosis, a viral infection which is characterized by atypical single-nucleus cells in the blood and which gives rise to a variety of symptoms. If you have ever suffered from the disease you will know that it can linger on for several months, during which one feels weak, feeble and thoroughly unwell.

I believe royal jelly may provide some measure of protection against catching this unpleasant disease since it contains the amino acid biotin as well as hydroxydecanoic acid with all its wonderful bactericidal, antibiotic and blood-conditioning properties. I know for certain that royal jelly's restorative powers can be invaluable during the later stages. The most remarkable report received in re-cent months concerning royal jelly and glandular fever came from a bubbly lass in her early 20s. She said,

> A few months ago I was a lethargic zombie suffering from glandular fever. I was too tired even to chew a pea or focus my eyes and couldn't imagine even having the strength to walk again...
>
> Within a few weeks of taking royal jelly I felt well enough to go on a tough walking holiday in Scotland with my friends. Armed with phials of liquid royal jelly I walked 15 miles a day, danced until the small hours, scaled the height of Ben Nevis and all on only 25 hours sleep in the week!

Almost in the same postbag I heard from someone who had been in an identical condition six weeks after having infectious mononucleosis diagnosed. This correspondent said, 'Within one week of taking one capsule a day of royal jelly I was feeling almost back to normal; after two weeks I am now back to my old former self.'

Headaches

Many users of royal jelly who frequently suffer from headaches report a reduced incidence of attacks while they are taking royal jelly. It is obvious that it would be helpful in treating the causes of tension and nervous headaches which affect a vast number of peo-ple in this fast-paced world. When used in conjunction with relaxa-tion techniques, royal jelly can make such headaches a thing of the past.

Hepatitis

There are many causes of hepatitis, which literally means 'inflammation of the liver'. As I mentioned at the beginning of this chapter, royal jelly is a standard treatment for any liver disorders, but particularly for hepatitis, in the Apitherapy Hospital at Lianyungang. I have not yet heard of it being used in this way in the West, but since royal jelly has been a standard cure for this condition for many years in China, I would be very interested in any future research along these lines.

Hyperactivity

I know of many mothers whose lives have been thrown into chaos by a hyperactive toddler or older child. It must be thoroughly nerve–racking to have to be constantly on the alert during the day and to continually have broken nights due to the very little sleep which such children require. Often, hyperactive children are extremely intelligent, making the intellectual demands on their mothers particularly taxing. There *are* drugs to control this condition, but few parents want to give their children strong medication when there are natural alternative remedies.

Because of its 'normalizing' action, royal jelly does not make hyperactive children even more full of energy: on the contrary, it has a considerable calming effect. Also, such children tend to have very short attention spans, and the glutamic acid, lysine and vitamin B12 in royal jelly can help here, too.

I recently heard from a very relieved mother who found that royal jelly did double duty for her hyperactive child; not only did it help to calm him but also cleared up the eczema to which many such children are prone.

> At first there was no change but gradually, after ten days, the eczema faded and didn't re-appear and he was going to sleep when he went to bed and waking up much later. His appetite improved and he seemed altogether *calmer*. Over the month the improvement has been maintained and there have been no further eczema attacks.

Hyperglycaemia and hypoglycaemia

As yet there is no evidence of royal jelly affecting either of these conditions dramatically, but the effect of the substance on blood sugar levels could well be a fruitful area of research, given the presence in royal jelly of an insulin-like peptide and the consistent normalizing action which royal jelly has on so many conditions. Also, glutamic acid and glycine deficiency can be a factor in both high and low blood sugar levels, and both these amino acids are present. Two other ingredients in royal jelly which could play a part in rectifying these conditions are pantothenic acid (a lack of which can induce hypoglycaemia) and chromium, a trace mineral which is often lacking in diabetics.

Hypertension and hypotension

In 1964 a Russian scientist observed the ability of royal jelly to lower high blood pressure and raise low blood pressure. Here is yet another instance of royal jelly's 'balancing' function, as it normalizes extremes in the body, whether these be physical or mental.

Impotence

Male impotence and female frigidity often involve a significant psychological factor. It is well known that stress can cause male impotence, but female 'impotence' cannot be measured quite so easily, for obvious reasons! However, there is a complaint in women which could be equated with stress-related male impotence and that is vaginismus, a contraction of the muscles of the vagina making it uncomfortable, if not physically impossible, for intercourse to take place. The key to curing stress-induced impotence in both sexes is, of course, relaxation or removal of the cause of the stress. This is not always possible, and in such cases royal jelly can prove helpful because of its calming effect on stressed and anxious men and women.

There are other ingredients in royal jelly which could help to remedy any physical cause for this condition. One is testosterone, which was detected in royal jelly in 1984. This hormone boosts the libido of both men and women. The amino acid phenylalanine, also present in royal jelly, performs the same function.

Insomnia

As we get older we need less sleep, but still many elderly people worry about the fact that they cannot sleep through the night. This is perfectly normal and the worst thing anyone suffering from sleeplessness can do is to lie in bed and fret. The best solution is to get up and make a soothing drink, or to do some household chores until your body tells you that it is time to sleep again. Of course, insomnia can be a cause for true concern when it is a symptom of some other disorder, such as stress or pain.

Royal jelly can relieve the stress, since it contains niacin and pyridoxine, both of which act as natural and non-habit-forming tranquillizers. It is interesting to look at the effect of royal jelly on animals with erratic sleeping patterns, as documented in Chapter 8. Pets which previously slept badly tend to sleep soundly, while those which once slept excessively remain awake for longer periods and are generally much more alert.

Kidney disorders

I referred to kidney problems in the section on Fluid retention since the two are often interrelated. I often hear of the beneficial effect of royal jelly on fluid retention, but I also receive letters from people who have found relief from both fluid retention and kidney problems. Mrs M. wrote,

> I have suffered with severe kidney pain intermittently since 1974, together with fluid retention, which caused unsightly 'bags' of water under my eyes, also permanent pains in the legs. Since taking royal jelly capsules my kidney pain is virtually nil. The water 'eye bags' have gone making me took ten years younger, and I haven't worn any tights or stockings this summer, when I thought I was doomed to wear support tights for the rest of my life.

Malnutrition

One would have though that no one in the West in our modern world ever had to worry about malnutrition, and we are constantly told that we get perfectly adequate nourishment from a normal balanced diet. It is true that anyone who eats sensibly is probably getting all the nourishment they require but there is one group in particular which is at risk of malnutrition and that is the elderly. If they are suffering from certain diseases of old age, such as senile dementia, or digestive problems, or simple depression, there may be no desire to eat at all, or the sufferer's diet may be woefully inadequate. The Loughborough trial with royal jelly and the elderly (described under Geriatric disorders) showed that appetites increased significantly and that all those in the trial felt very much better for their course of capsules.

That royal jelly is a highly nutritious substance was demonstrated in 1966 during trials in France and Italy with malnourished and underweight infants. The reports indicated that the subjects' appetites were stimulated in almost all cases and that weight gain was clearly visible within 20 days. Laboratory tests revealed that red corpuscle counts were increased and assimilation of protein into the bloodstream was greater than that induced by other known treatments of malnutrition.

Menopausal symptoms

Approximately 70 per cent of women experience embarrassing and very uncomfortable 'hot flushes' during the menopause. Irritability and depression are also common symptoms. Both anxiety and depression respond to royal jelly, as I have mentioned elsewhere, but the substance also seems to treat the vascular disturbances which cause the flushes. One of my correspondents told me, 'I am 51 years of age and in the midst of the change of life...hot flushes are a thing of the past for me, thanks to royal jelly.'

I firmly believe that royal jelly is a great help to women during the menopause and I would love to hear from anyone who has experienced its benefits during that time. I should be particularly interested to hear of anyone who has found relief from symptoms while taking royal jelly and has then stopped taking the capsules, and has then experienced a return of the disturbances.

Morning sickness

Much play was made in the press of the story that Her Royal Highness the Princess of Wales took royal jelly to ward off morning sickness when she was expecting both Prince William and Prince Harry. The fact that she used royal jelly during her second pregnancy implies that it was helpful during the first, and if this is so she would not be alone in finding relief through taking a daily capsule. A midwife in Dublin recommends royal jelly to all the expectant mums in her ante-natal classes so that their pregnancies can be free of nausea, following her good experiences with royal jelly capsules during her own two pregnancies.

Multiple sclerosis

I should be delighted to hear from anyone with multiple sclerosis who is taking royal jelly, as I believe that royal jelly could prove helpful in treating this disease. MS attacks the protective myelin sheaths which insulate nerve fibres at various points around the central nervous system. Royal jelly contains the amino acid aspartic acid, and the trace mineral silicon, both of which protect the nervous system.

It is also thought that multiple sclerosis might be a malfunction of the immune system and royal jelly has plenty of ingredients which can help to bring the immune system to peak condition. I know that many sufferers have great faith in oil of evening primrose, and royal jelly shares similar properties. Taking royal jelly will certainly not harm those with multiple sclerosis, and it is bound at least to improve their overall health and lift their spirits.

Muscular dystrophy

This is yet another disease which is not yet fully understood. It is thought to be due to congenital errors of metabolism. Whatever the case, royal jelly offers two ingredients which are used in standard treatments of this progressive disease: vitamin B12 and the amino acid glycine, which boosts muscle function. In my last book I quoted a letter from a muscular dystrophy sufferer who found that, although taking royal jelly did not seem to affect the progress of her disease, she believed it helped her greatly by reducing her susceptibility to colds and coughs.

Myalgic encephalomyelitis

It is only in the last couple of years that this disease (usually referred to as ME since its full name is such a mouthful) has been recognized. Probably the most famous sufferer was Clare Francis, the author and once a record-breaking yachtswoman, but many people all over the world are struggling with ME. It often takes months before a firm diagnosis is made, which does nothing to help the severely depressed patient. As yet there is not much that the medical profession can do to help, because ME is not yet fully understood. In fact, ME is so shrouded in mystery and lack of understanding that it goes under a variety of other names, including Chronic Fatigue Syndrome (CFS for short), yuppie 'flu, chronic Epstein-Barr syndrome and post-viral fatigue. It has not yet been proven beyond doubt that these are one and the same disease, but they certainly share many symptoms — chronic fatigue, digestive problems, depression, difficulty in concentrating and skeletal pain. Although individual symptoms may respond to medical treatment, the patient usually has to just wait until he or she gets better, which may take years rather than months.

I have received several letters from sufferers reporting impressive results from taking royal jelly daily. Steve Wilkinson, author of *ME and You* (Thorsons, 1988), went so far as to carry out his own trial with a group of ten ME patients. His enthusiasm was kindled, following the increased mental function and lifting of depression which he experienced after treating his own ME with royal jelly.

The ten participants in the trial took 450 mg of royal jelly daily for six months. After the first three months there was an involuntary gap of two weeks in the treatment while new supplies were awaited. This period of 'withdrawal' proved very informative since symptoms which had disappeared during the first part of the trial were beginning to return with a vengeance by the second week of the break.

However, once the royal jelly arrived and the patients resumed their daily doses, the symptoms began to recede again. In the fourth month and thereafter, many participants felt so much better that they began to overestimate their own abilities, undertaking much more energetic projects. This led to some setbacks, but more sensible activity patterns soon solved the problem.

By the end of the trial, all ten participants were showing marked signs of physical, mental and emotional improvement. They had more stamina and physical strength, and improved powers of memory and concentration. They also suffered less from mood swings.

There was some problem with the dosage at first, as 450 mg proved too much for some participants initially. Steve recommends increasing the dosage gradually from 150 to 450 mg per day over a six-week period to avoid any adverse reactions.

One patient was in a wheelchair at the outset but, within four months, was fit enough to return to school. Others were bedridden to begin with and were slowly able to adopt a more active lifestyle.

Steve ended his report on the trial,

> Royal jelly is a safe and effective treatment for myalgic encephalomyelitis. It reduces the severity of all the major symptoms in the short and medium term, and in the long term seems to act as a remedial agent. It has been shown to prevent the normal pattern of relapses common to sufferers of this illness, and speeds recovery times when relapses do occur due to over-activity. It enables even the most severely affected sufferers to return to a near-normal lifestyle when used over a period of six months or longer.

In America, Dr Richard Gerber has recently produced a paper entitled 'The Use of Royal Jelly in the Treatment of Chronic Fatigue Syndrome'. (As I mentioned earlier, Chronic Fatigue Syndrome or CFS is just one of ME's aliases.) In his paper, Dr Gerber reports on a pilot study carried out with six carefully selected patients. All had to fit the classic picture of a CFS sufferer and had to have failed to respond to Dr Gerber's previous treatment with vitamin supplements.

The six patients ranged in age from 25–75 years and all experienced fatigue as their worst problem. They were instructed to continue with their established medical and vitamin treatment, but to supplement this with one fresh royal jelly capsule daily. If this proved insufficient to have any effect on their energy levels, they were to double their intake of royal jelly.

Dr Gerber reports,

> All six patients observed significant improvements in their energy level and activity tolerance. Half the patients were im-

proved on one capsule of royal jelly daily, while the other half required two capsules. One patient was able to finally work a normal day at her job without being totally exhausted. Other patients, including one severe cardiac patient, were able to increase their activity tolerance to do more exercise and walking up to three miles daily, where before this had been limited to only half a mile. While these results are preliminary, they are indeed promising.

Post-natal depression

The 'baby blues' are experienced by most mothers to a certain extent when, a few days after giving birth, levels of the various hormones are shifting up and down to settle in the correct relationship for a non-pregnant women who is breastfeeding. Unfortunately, for some mums this period of depression can last several months and may even continue for years after the birth. The symptoms are not unlike those of pre-menstrual syndrome and it must be terrible for anyone who has to live with such severe depression, irritability and even suicidal tendencies for such a long time.

Fortunately, royal jelly cannot only help to lift the depression; it can also give the new mum the extra energy she requires to look after the new arrival and improve her general health so that she can cope better with her illness. A second-time mother wrote to me recently, saying, 'I am convinced the royal jelly has kept me healthy and able to cope.'

Pre-menstrual syndrome

Pre-menstrual tension has been known to wreck marriages and even lead to violence. I fear that it is still not taken seriously enough by the medical profession. In the past, doctors may have been confounded by the wide variety of symptoms associated with the syndrome and, although they could releive the 'bloatedness' with diuretics, the irritability, depression and irrationality proved more difficult to treat. It has been found that vitamin B6 is helpful in relieving the mental symptoms, as is oil of evening primrose. Royal jelly, since it contains most the the B vitamins — including B6 — has proved invaluable for many women. Typical comments are, 'I have found that my PMT is eradicated', 'at no time did I get any depression, which in itself was a miracle!' An added bonus is that royal jelly acts as a natural diuretic so, with luck, it can cope with all the unpleasant symptoms of pre-menstrual syndrome.

Psoriasis

This non-contagious skin disease causes considerable discomfort and stress to sufferers who, because the lesions are unsightly, prefer to cover affected areas. Because of this, the layman tends to imagine that it is a fairly rare complaint, but in fact approximately 1 person in 50 is plagued by it. Since stress can precipitate fresh lesions, people with psoriasis are often trapped in a vicious circle of stress and psoriasis, with new outbreaks causing more stress which causes the psoriasis to worsen. Happily, as with so many skin conditions, the relevant active ingredients in royal jelly, pantothenic acid, phosphorus, sulphur, riboflavin, niacin and biotin, can come to the rescue. It does not seem to matter whether the substance is applied externally to the affected parts by means of a cream or taken internally in the form of capsules — the result is the same. A typical response is reported by Mrs H.

> I had psoriasis on my arms, hands and parts of my body for a considerable time. None of the prescribed creams helped. Within three months [of taking royal jelly capsules] it has disappeared. I feel better, able to cope with stress much better...

Another correspondent wrote to me of a 'tremendous improvement in the psoriasis, which I have had on and off for over 40 years!' She too was prepared to persevere with the capsules for three months, since it is clear that a condition which has been unaffected by all the weapons in the medical armoury will not vanish overnight, however effective the eventual cure may be.

Scleroderma

This is a rare but very distressing and progressive disease, thought to be an immunological disorder, of which the outward signs are a hardening and tightening of the skin. Internally, the disease affects the connective tissues of the colon, lungs and kidneys and can even reach the heart.

Unfortunately, there is no known cure for this debilitating illness, but several sufferers have found that royal jelly cream is very beneficial for any ulcers which develop, while taken internally, it does its usual effective job of boosting spirits and imparting a feeling of well-being. Indeed, the President of the Maria Scleroderma Therapy Trust, Elvira Smith, recommends royal jelly to her members.

Stress

Stress, in the right quantities, does not lead to ill health; on the contrary it can be very energizing. However, when the pressures of life exceed a certain limit (which varies from person to person), anxiety or depression can result. 'Stress management' is a modern 'buzz' phrase, but it makes sense, if we are suffering, to try to remove any unnecessary stresses from our lives and to put aside time every day for relaxation.

However, there are some circumstances, for example, bereavement, divorce, even Christmas, when it is extremely difficult to 'manage' the stress and the beleaguered may need help if they are to survive the experience without suffering too much mental trauma.

Relief from depression and anxiety is a commonly reported result of taking royal jelly and a welcome relief it is when the whole world seems bleak and black. Mrs H. from Middlesex reported,

> When my husband died five years ago after a long illness I really had a breakdown. When a friend recommended royal jelly I decided to try it and found it such a help: my whole outlook was changed, I had more energy and felt better totally. I can only say it helped me tremendously through the trauma of bereavement.

Another correspondent wrote,

> I went through a period of stress in which I felt as if everything was rush, rush, and I also seemed as if I had no patience for anyone, including my young son. My doctor prescribed a mild tranquillizer, but I didn't like that idea. I purchased some royal jelly capsules and, after three months, I feel on top of the world.

Stroke

Little is known of the underlying cause of the cerebral haemorrhage which we know as a stroke, but there is a strong association with hypertension (raised blood pressure) and royal jelly has been seen to be effective in lowering blood pressure where this is required.

Sub-fertility

Failure to conceive can be due to all manner of physical causes, but it is always possible that there is some dietary deficiency. We know that women must have adequate supplies of folic acid in their system before conception can occur, and a lack of the amino acid arginine can result in a low sperm count. Both are present in royal jelly, so it is well worth trying if a man's sperm count needs to be increased, or if no other reason for failure to conceive can be found.

I have heard of several cases of menopausal women conceiving and of couples who have tried in vain to start a family succeeding after a course of royal jelly. A proud grandmother wrote to me about her daughter and son-in-law who had tried for 14 years to have a child.

In August 1985 they both decided to take royal jelly to help them through the winter months with no thoughts of ever becoming pregnant (they had given up hope of having a family). However, on New Year's Day of 1986 Pamela was confirmed as pregnant, and in August 1986 she had a beautiful baby girl.

Two years later, the couple had another daughter, when the mother was 40 years old. Of course, it may well be that conception occurred because the couple had decided that they were destined never to have children — it often happens that once people have come to terms with infertility, the longed-for baby arrives! However, royal jelly may have had a part to play, and at the very least it will have helped the mother through her pregnancy and hopefully will have protected her from post-natal depression.

I received a similar letter from a lady in Greece who had taken royal jelly capsules to cure her acne. She and her husband had been trying for a baby for seven years and had twice been accepted for 'in vitro' fertilization, but even this had not resulted in the longed-for conception. Four months after she started taking royal jelly capsules, Mrs S. became pregnant.

Before the Duke and Duchess of York conceived their daughter, Princess Beatrice, there were press reports that the couple were taking large doses of royal jelly to increase their chances of starting a family. It was even said that the Duchess was taking massive doses of liquid royal jelly tonic with this aim in view. If this story is correct, she obviously fared very well on her bee's milk diet, but I would not advise every sub-fertile woman to follow her example; the normal royal jelly capsule regime should suffice!

Tranquillizer addiction

Decades ago, when modern tranquillizers were first prescribed, no one realized the trouble which was being stored up for the future. In the late 1980s, many middle-aged (and younger) people who have been taking tranquillizers for years are trying to live without them and suffering the most dreadful withdrawal symptoms. I would not dream of suggesting that anyone try to stop taking tranquillizers without medical supervision, but since royal jelly has so many naturally calming and stress-relieving properties, it might well prove a boon at such a time.

For one of my American correspondents who was taking royal jelly to combat the side-effects of chemotherapy and radiation, being able to cut down her tranquillizer dose came as a very pleasant surprise. She told me, 'One of the most amazing things that has happened to me is that I have been taking Valium for 30 years (15 mg per day). I am delighted to say that since taking my royal jelly, I am now taking only 2.5 mg sometimes at bedtime.'

———————— ...and in health ————————

You will have gathered from the preceding pages that royal jelly is an invaluable aid in the treatment of a multitude of ailments, but for me its chief value lies in its preventive properties. I would much rather take royal jelly and not fall ill than wait until I need its curative powers for one illness or another!

Similarly, we may feel perfectly healthy, but I have often heard of people who did not realize that they were not perfectly fit until they experienced the metamorphosis brought about by taking royal jelly. The extra energy and indefinable 'glow' which characterize a royal jelly user are something to behold, I can assure you. Royal jelly can have the most remarkable effects on users' appearance. I have already mentioned several times the benefits to skin, hair and nails, but there is one bonus which I have not discussed in much detail, and that is the youthful quality of those people who take royal jelly regularly.

Ageing

We all have to grow old, I know, but with royal jelly it is possible to retain our youthful exuberance and appearance for longer. It is not the elixir of youth, but so many people who use royal jelly are often thought to be much younger than they are. My mother Sophie is a case in point: now in her late 70s, she could pass for fifteen years younger. 'I have been using royal jelly for the past twenty years — am now aged 70 — my friends say I look half this age'; 'I will be 65 in January and no one believes me'; 'Initial reactions are ones of surprise when I mention my age...this I am sure is due to royal jelly, it certainly seems to slow down the ageing process'; 'People take me for my daughter's sister': these are just some of the comments I have received from more mature users of royal jelly.

Is there any reason why royal jelly should have this effect? Well, there are ingredients which could contribute to such a result. The amino acid glutamic acid is known to delay ageing, while pantothenic acid helps to prevent premature grey hairs. However, I think the most potent source of a youthful appearance is a happy disposition and boundless energy. I have noticed that people who take royal jelly seem to have an abundance of both of these.

Baldness

I mentioned the balding gentleman whose hair is starting to grow again in Chapter Two. I have heard of a couple of cases of hair regeneration, and there are two ingredients in royal jelly which are needed to prevent premature balding, the amino acid lysine and biotin. However, it may be that these gentlemen were losing their hair as a reaction to stress and that royal jelly, with its calming properties, gave their hair follicles the breathing space in which to produce new growth.

Pregnancy

I have included pregnancy in the 'healthy' section deliberately. So many pregnant women tell me that they are treated as though they had an illness during their pregnancy and during childbirth when, in truth, they have never felt so healthy before in their lives. One can understand and sympathize with the attitude of the medical profession since their sole aim is to ensure that pregnancy and childbirth are trouble-free and result in a healthy baby, but the first-time mother in particular can feel somewhat nervous and intimidated, when faced with so many tests and examinations during the ante-natal period and so much high technology in the delivery room.

Royal jelly can play an important role in every pregnancy, ensuring that both mother and baby receive the best possible nutrition, that blood pressure is kept down, that morning sickness is kept at bay and that, after the birth, the mother has the extra energy and the anxiety-free days which she needs if those first few months are to be as happy and fulfilling as they should be. A proud father-to-be wrote,

> My wife is expected a baby in January. She started taking royal jelly capsules at the beginning of October, she feels generally well, hair is better and fingernails are stronger, and my wife has noticed that her weight has increased slightly compared with our first baby, but also she is more relaxed and her nerves are much better now...

Protection against infection

On the preventive front again, 'I never seem to catch a cold', 'I don't seem to catch anything any more', are typical comments from royal jelly users. There may never be a cure for the common cold, given the multiplicity of different viruses which the word 'cold' embraces, but the development of antibodies which is encouraged by the pyrodoxine and biotin in royal jelly can come to our defence when cold germs surround us, and the overall good health which royal jelly imparts must also aid resistance to infection from these and other viruses.

I should like to end this chapter with the story of a remarkable 71-year-old gentleman who wrote to me recently. In 1965 he had heart surgery, followed 15 years later by surgery for a stomach problem. In the following year, 1981, he suffered four strokes, then in 1987 had bronchitis and pernicious anaemia. After taking a capsule of royal jelly each day his health improved tremendously; so much so that he pronounced royal jelly 'the most remarkable discovery since Rutherford split the atom!'

CHAPTER 8

——Silent testimony——

When I wrote *Royal Jelly: A guide to nature's richest health food* I reported on the initial results of a relatively recent introduction — fresh royal jelly for animals. Since that time, royal jelly has taken the animal world by storm. Its fame has spread mostly by word of mouth but also, I am glad to relate, through the veterinary profession. I must confess myself mystified at this strange difference in attitude between doctors who treat humans and those who treat animals. I have heard of few cases of an orthodox medical practitioner recommending royal jelly to one of his patients, but I have heard of many cases of vets not only showing an interest in the substance but also suggesting it as a treatment for poorly pets.

Mr Richard Allport, a Member of the Royal College of Veterinary Surgeons, is so impressed by royal jelly that he takes it himself, recommends it to the pet owners who come to his surgery and has even carried out some trials. His first trial was an informal one with groups of cats to assess suitable dose rates. Even in this trial two cats showed startling improvements in chronic health problems from which they were suffering. One cat with long-term conjunctivitis improved greatly while being given royal jelly. Another cat needing frequent injections for a persistent gum inflammation required much less intensive treatment while taking part in the trial. Then Mr Allport decided to try replicating the results of the Egyptian rat trial reported in Chapter 5. For this particular trial he used young rabbits in place of the immature rats.

You will remember that the Egyptian scientists were attempting to evaluate the effects of fresh royal jelly and freeze-dried royal jelly on the growth rates of immature rats, compared with the growth rate of rats who were given a 'placebo'. They concluded that royal jelly in both forms significantly accelerated maturity, but that fresh royal jelly was markedly more effective in this respect.

Overall, Mr Allport's trial seemed to bear out the Egyptian findings in that those rabbits receiving royal jelly put on weight much more quickly than the control group. Interestingly, in the first week of the trial the effect was quite dramatic, the group given royal jelly putting on over 40 per cent more weight than their counterparts. As the trial progressed, a weight differential was maintained, but only in the first week was the increase in weight so astounding. I asked Richard whether he had reached any conclusions about this disparity in growth rate.

'My feeling is', he told me, 'that the big difference noted in the early stages was due to the calming effect of royal jelly. When the trial began, the rabbits had just been weaned and moved to a completely new and strange environment, They must have been suffering from stress for the first week or so. Perhaps the royal jelly lessened the effects of the stress, enabling that group of rabbits to accelerate their growth rate, while the progress of those rabbits which were not given royal jelly was temporarily impeded by the stress factor.'

Further trials are now under way. A breeding trial has just been completed, and the initial results show that a group of breeding does given royal jelly, produced more rabbits per litter, with higher birthweights than a similar group not given royal jelly. Another growth rate trial is in progress, to confirm the results of the original work.

It will be fascinating to see the full results of all these trials, and of those currently being undertaken involving racing pigeons, racehorses and greyhounds. Whatever the outcome, Richard is convinced of the benefits of royal jelly to animals. 'It works, of that I have no doubt', he said, 'I feel the ingredients of royal jelly may have a synergistic effect. In other words, the total effect of the vitamins, minerals and other elements in royal jelly taken together is greater than the sum of their separate individual effects.'

─────────── Recent advances ───────────

It seems logical that since cats, dogs and horses are different species, their requirements from a dietary supplement are also different. For this reason, three new types of royal jelly capsules have appeared on the market recently, one for each species. These capsules have, of course, been formulated with the requirements of each type of animal in mind.

The capsules for dogs each contain 100 mg fresh royal jelly with similar preservatives to those used in the 'human' capsules, but with the addition of halibut liver oil, a natural source of vitamins A and D. Also included are beeswax and lecithin which act as natural stabilizers and emusifiers.

Horses, being very much larger animals, are given 500 mg fresh royal jelly in each capsule, again preserved in honey and wheatgerm oil, two ingredients which enhance the effects of fresh royal jelly. The same quantity of spirulina has been included. This is a highly concentrated natural food supplement derived from blue-green algae found growing in the world's oceans. It is higher in protein than any other natural food, and is rich in vitamins, minerals and essential fatty acids.

Since cats are the smallest of these three animal types, each of their capsules contains 50 mg royal jelly, blended with honey, wheatgerm oil and halibut liver oil. The feline formulation contains a much larger proportion of halibut liver oil than the canine capsule, since it is believed that cats are more likely to be deficient in vitamins A and D than dogs are.

Also available for each species is a specially formulated version of liquid fresh royal jelly tonic for occasional use only. I shall be very interested to hear how owners and breeders fare with these three new product ranges. Since each has been specially designed for a particular species, I should expect that even more startling results will be achieved with the new products than have already been achieved with the all-purpose animal royal jelly capsules.

Being a cat owner myself, I of course want our pets to benefit from all the wonderful properties of royal jelly, but I keep a close eye on the results of giving the substance to animals for another reason. There is a school of thought which holds that virtually any illness (including disorders such as gallstones, arthritis and cancer) has psychosomatic roots and can be cured simply by an alteration in the patient's mental attitude. It could be said that faith-healing relies on this premise for its effectiveness. Whether this tenet has any basis in fact or not, it is an argument frequently used by sceptics when remarkable 'cures' are reported after unorthodox treatments have been given to patients.

There is no doubt that there is frequently a psychological element in recovery from illness. For example, it has been found that cancer patients can improve their chances of recovery by adopting an optimistic and determined attitude of mind. Then again, if you take any medicine in the firm belief that it will help you, the odds are that you will notice an improvement in your condition, even if that medicine is just a sugar pill!

For this reason, animals are an important source of objective evidence on the effectiveness of royal jelly. They are not capable of associating their daily treat with any physical condition from which they are suffering. Improvement in such conditions is therefore not influenced by psychological factors, although we still have to bear in mind the attitude of the animals' owners. It is possible for a loving owner who is convinced of the merits of royal jelly to see imagined improvements. Or perhaps the owner is giving the pet more attention in a subconscious attempt to 'will' the royal jelly to work. The pet may well thrive with this increased attention and improve much more rapidly than otherwise.

I am therefore particularly interested in the opinions of breeders and other professionals in the animal world as they are more likely to be clinically objective in their assessments of the value of royal jelly. Consequently, you will find that many of the case histories in this chapter come from owners who are 'in the profession': vets, owners of show animals, breeders, pet shop owners, etc. I have also included reports from pet owners whose animals have been suffering from specific, objectively assessable disorders, so that my readers may have a full picture of the range of results produced by royal jelly when it is given to animals.

However, many reports come in from owners of more unusual animals. Mrs. H., for example, has a wild bird and animal hospital in Kent, and she wrote to tell me the extraordinary tale of the Vertical Take-Off Bat.

> Last Friday, I was handed an adult male long-eared bat, It had been trapped in a lounge for at least two days and was generally weak with hunger, thirst and exhaustion. I mixed 0.25 ml royal jelly tonic with 0.5 ml skimmed milk and allowed the bat to drink some of this mixture. Approximately five minutes after drinking this the most amazing thing happened. He actually jumped in the air and started flying around inside our house! I was told by the Flora and Fauna Society at London Zoo that bats need to be 'hung up' on a vertical surface for approximately 20 minutes to 'wind themselves up' before flight can take place.
>
> I can't wait to get another bat in to try royal jelly tonic again!

Mrs H. has had equally startling results feeding fresh royal jelly and honey to an anorexic cockatoo and royal jelly tonic to a similarly afflicted young tortoise. Both regained their appetites, put on weight and flourished.

Pigeon-fanciers also swear by royal jelly. A keen pigeon-racer recently entered two pigeons fed on royal jelly for a race from France to England. Only 30 of the 1,929 birds which left France arrived home that same day and the two royal jelly pigeons flew in first and fourth!

I have even been contacted by a lady who keep lizards. It seems that lizards are prone to mouth ulcers which spread all over the body and eventually prove fatal. This correspondent was intending to treat her lizards with royal jelly in an attempt to arrest if not cure the condition, and I look forward to hearing about the results of this rather unusual application!

Before embarking on case studies of more familiar pets, such as cats and dogs, I should like to quote in full a letter I received from

Nancy H., since it shows how royal jelly can help animals in sickness *and* in health!

> Two and a half months ago I put our four cats on royal jelly. The eldest who is ten suffers from arthritis especially in the damp and cold weather. After getting up from sleeping she would limp, and naturally when she was in pain would be somewhat grumpy and snappy. Last winter she was put on steroids by the vet to help her. However, after two and a half months on royal jelly what a difference! No limping — she obviously feels much better as her temperament has greatly improved.

> Our 4-year-old cat suffers from feline urinology syndrome and has to take daily medication. On royal jelly he has really perked up, brighter eyes, better appetite, etc. I am trying to cut his medication down slightly, and no doubt with the help of royal jelly will succeed.

> Our two younger cats, 19 months and 7 months, were very healthy to start with but we couldn't leave them out! On royal jelly their coats are a credit to them, they both look and feel shiny, sleek and beautiful.

From this account and from the accounts which follow you will realize that the effects of royal jelly on humans are mirrored in animals: dramatic improvements in arthritis, better hair and skin (read 'coats' for animals!), relief of insomnia, speedy recovery after surgery, increased energy and so on. To me, this means that we have to take claims for improvements in equivalent conditions in people very seriously.

Boxer dog and bitch — temperament problems

Kay White is a freelance journalist with the healthy measure of scepticism which is one of the hallmarks of a good journalist. She confesses that she was 'a bit blasé about supplements' and that she started her two boxers on royal jelly 'with minimal expectations'. Kay was in for a pleasant surprise!

Jemima, the young bitch, was a very shy dog with no town experience and prone to be 'spooky' when away from familiar surroundings, so it was with some trepidation that Kay took her on a two-week touring holiday. Much to Kay's astonishment, Jemima 'behaved like the most sophisticated dog in the world. Controlled, poised and charming, she won praise even from hoteliers who did not usually allow dogs on their premises.' Kay wondered whether the royal jelly was working as a tranquillizer, but rejected the idea since Jemima was still full of bounce and was eating heartily.

Meanwhile, back home, Pip was being looked after by 'sitters'. He is normally an aggressive dog when near other animals, nourishing 'the ambition to be the last dog left alive' — so much so that Kay advised the sitters not to take him out. However, the sitters obtained a very different impression of Pip and disregarded Kay's advice: he behaved perfectly for the two weeks on twice-daily walks. Says Kay,

> I am still amazed at the effect on the dogs, because at the time of giving the capsules I was quite unaware of what the product could do. Had I been expecting a personality change to be created in the dogs I might be wondering if I had deluded myself that it had indeed taken place, but nothing was further from my mind. Now the knowledge has been forced upon me that their personalities can be modified up or down according to their individial needs by something as simple and elemental as bee food.

Chihuahua dog — emphysema/constipation

Poor Rupert was almost 9 years old when his owner, Mrs F., took him to the vet who diagnosed emphysema, tracheitis and a heart condition. He had a continuous cough and, although various drugs were tried, there was little improvement in his condition. Then, two years later, Mrs F. started Rupert on a course of royal jelly, having been recommended it by a fellow dog owner. From the time that the Chihuahua started to take royal jelly, he was given no drugs at all. Within three months there was a remarkable improvement: his breathing was less laboured, he coughed much less and his stiff joints seemed to have eased. Rupert had also suffered from constipation, for which Mrs F. had previously been giving him medication. To Mrs F.'s delight, the constipation eased, too. As an added bonus, the dog's coat has improved, his eyes are brighter and he is more interested in life. 'It is marvellous to have Rupert off drugs. My husband and I are still amazed at his improvement', said Mrs F.

Corgi dog — cystitis

Corgi breeders Mr and Mrs B. had to hand-rear Ben and Tanya as there were serious whelping problems. As a very young puppy, Ben suffered several bouts of cystitis. When the two pups were 4 months old, they began a royal jelly regime: 'Knowing the benefits of royal jelly for humans, I put them on it as early as possible', said Mr B. Ben and Tanya are now 20 months olds with several Championship and Open Show wins and places to their credit. In 16 months of taking royal jelly, Ben has been completely free of cystitis.

English Setter dog — congenital liver malfunction

Angela Bryant is a pet shop proprietor who bought a 14-week-old English Setter, called Jeeves, for herself. Jeeves was a little thin when Angela took him home, but she was sure that all he needed was good food and attention. However, the puppy's condition deteriorated and the vet eventually diagnosed a congenital liver disorder with an associated intestinal infection. It was thought unlikely that Jeeves would live past 6 months of age and, even if he did, he would never make the show ring.

Angela then heard about royal jelly capsules for animals and decided to give them a try.

> Any extra intake of the normal vitamins one would normally give to a developing pup would have antagonized the problem. So, with careful diet, the medication prescribed from the vet and, of course, royal jelly, we have progressed better than the vet or myself could possibly have hoped for.
>
> Jeeves is now over 10 months old — healthy, lively (why did I ever moan that he was too quiet?) — just about normal weight and if I say so myself, in lovely condition.

This lovely Setter has had two show outings so far, winning 1st English Setter Puppy at Open Show level the first time, and V.H.C. in English Setter Puppy Dog at the Manchester Championship show the second time. Angela is sure that Jeeves has a sparkling show career ahead of him, which is a wonderful outcome considering that he came so close to death's door in those early months. Incidentally, royal jelly was not solely responsible for Jeeves' showring success — he is brother to the 1988 Crufts Supreme Champion!

Bloodhound bitch — nervousness

Emma was 2 years old and was always very nervy. She had been frightened by fireworks and was subsequently nervous of men, loud noises, strangers, lorries and cars — in fact she was worried about anything strange to her. Within a couple of months of beginning a course of royal jelly capsules her nerves had dramatically improved. Mrs D., her owner, reported, 'She greets strangers, trots with her tail up, is happy and contented, calmed down, and is still improving.' Other benefits were a beautiful shiny coat and better sleeping patterns.

Cat — kidney disease

A lady who had achieved remarkable results herself with liquid royal jelly tonic, decided to give the animal capsules to her 16-year-old cat, suffering from kidney disease. She was more than delighted with the result: 'To look at his shiny coat, youthful appearance and having a "mad" session every day, running up and down stairs, dashing from room to room, you would think he was a kitten!'

Cairn Terrier dog — skin allergy

Toffee had been suffering from a skin problem for some time and was receiving antibiotics from the vet when his owner, Miss W., decided to try him on royal jelly. 'The vet heartily endorsed my giving him royal jelly', says Miss W., 'and he is now clear of skin problems.' The beneficial 'side-effects' of the royal jelly treatment came as a bonus: Toffee changed from being lethargic and sleepy to being a lively and generally much happier dog, with a better appetite and 'a very soft and shiny coat'.

Bloodhound bitch — no appetite

Sybil showed very little interest in food and sometimes fasted for weeks at a time. When her owner, Mrs E., tried giving Sybil royal jelly capsules, the result was too good to be true: 'Six seconds after I gave her the royal jelly she started eating — this must have been coincidental'. Indeed it must have been, but two months later, the bitch was considerably improved. She was eating regularly with a hearty appetite and, even though she had always been a lively dog, she now had even more energy. Mrs E. summed the results up very vividly: 'It's as if she's had a good holiday!'

Unspecified breed — slipped disc

Sue B. was having problems with her dog who was becoming very bored and naughty from having to keep still and lead a quiet life six weeks after slipping a disc. She was thrilled with the improvement after starting him on a course of royal jelly capsules.

'My dog has improved in leaps and bounds and is now running about — though with some lack of co-ordination; but his zest for life is wonderful. My vet has said he is interested in the effect, particularly as he is still improving.'

Three Cocker Spaniels — lethargy/lack of confidence/loss of appetite

Mrs M., a Cocker Spaniel breeder from Leicestershire, reported the remarkable effects of the capsules on three of her show dogs. A 21-month-old dog who was growing lethargic came back to win a Reserve C.C.; a bitch who would not show, through lack of confidence, has 'come out of her shell'; and a 10-month-old bitch who was off her food returned to eating three meals a day. 'I am sure it is the capsules that have done this', wrote Mrs M. 'It is too much of a coincidence for three dogs to improve in different ways at the same time.'

Rottweiler dog — anorexia nervosa

Talas was a good eater as a young puppy, but he went off his food at the age of 7 months and developed anorexia nervosa. His owner, Mrs D., spent a fortune on appetizers and concentrates but with no success. 'We had almost given up, and thought about taking him out of the ring until we tried one last time with royal jelly and we couldn't believe it. Tal had been taking the capsules for two days when we noticed his appetite had increased. It's brilliant.'

Shi-tzu bitch — mammary tumours/no coat

Gladys S. owns 11-year-old Panda who came to her in a very poor condition at twenty months old. The Shi-tzu had no coat at all and, although Gladys built her up with a good diet, the coat would not grow to any great length. Then Panda developed mammary tumours, one of which suddenly enlarged. The vet was able to remove the large growth but felt that Panda could not survive the removal of the others, so left them. When Mrs S. took the patient home, she gave her two capsules of royal jelly a day. The results were soon to show. 'Her coat is now lovely and thick and long — and *feels* in good condition', writes Gladys. 'She is also much more lively and energetic and her appetite has really improved.'

Irish Water Spaniel dog — severe depression

Thomas was wasting away after losing his kennel mate. The vet tried different drugs with no success. The spaniel had completely lost interest in living and was having to be force-fed. In desperation, his owner tried royal jelly capsules.

Thomas was very thin and had virtually no body coat and huge bare patches on his shoulders and hindquarters where he lay on his side for great lengths of time. We also had to turn him over regularly to keep his circulation going. After five days of taking the capsules, he actually got up and walked around and looked for something to eat. That day he had two small meals which he ate by himself. Improvement has been steady from then on.

Cavalier King Charles Spaniel dog — heart murmur/no appetite/lacklustre eyes/lethargy

Rupert had had considerable success in Championship Shows on the Continent, being a triple champion and once Reserve Best in Show. However, when he came out of quarantine after one of his cross-Channel trips it was found that he had a heart murmur and he had to be force-fed. After three days on royal jelly 'his eyes became bright and very shiny' declared his owner, Julia G. 'By the fifth day he pulled himself up and strutted around full of himself — my champion had returned.' Rupert began eating by himself and his appetite became if anything too healthy as Julia had to restrict his intake of biscuits. The nervousness which had plagued him following an attack by an Irish Wolfhound began to evaporate, and from being lethargic and sleepy, Rupert became 'much more wakeful, very much "on guard" and full of bounce and vitality.' Julia admits, 'I tried the capsules in desperation, never really expecting such excellent results.'

Miniature Dachshund bitch — immune system breakdown

Ada had been very ill over a long period 'with one thing after another going wrong', says her owner. She was so ill that the vet had to see her daily if her life was to be saved. As soon as she started taking royal jelly capsules the improvements began to show. Her appetite increased, her coat which had once been dry now had a smooth, glossy sheen, and she recovered her zest for life. 'She is a joy to us all', reports her thankful owner.

There are many other cases which I could mention. A dog who was badly mauled, sustaining severed tendons, lacerations and bites, recovered completely after an operation and a course of royal jelly. 'If anything she is too lively!' says her proud owner. A highly-strung Afghan puppy that once suffered from travel sickness started to eat regularly and calmed down after only six weeks' treatment. A King Charles Spaniel that used to shake on the judge's table and sometimes collapse, took royal jelly for 12 days after which he was behaving perfectly and the colour of his coat was improving.

Whenever I talk to pet owners who have tried royal jelly I hear the same stories. One of the most surprising features is that animals seem to respond to these capsules even more quickly than humans and in many cases the improvements are even more dramatic. Could this be because we humans sometimes mistrust any signs of improvement in ourselves and cling to our illnesses out of a sense of perversity? I wonder!

I am pleased to say, given my own conviction that there is

nothing to better it for either ourselves or our animal friends, that more and more pets all over the world are beginning to enjoy the benefits which a royal jelly regime can bring. I recently met Her Serene Highness Princess Antoinette of Monaco, who is Vice President of the Kennel Club of Great Britain. I have already mentioned that the Monegasque royal family are royal jelly enthusiasts, but I was delighted to learn that the royal dogs are not left out when it comes to the daily round of capsules!

CHAPTER 9

—————— Almost there ——————

Three years ago, when *Royal Jelly: A guide to nature's richest health food* was published, I was optimistic that royal jelly would gain acceptance by the medical community as a standard preliminary treatment. I still have that hope and it seems as though doctors are, at least, more willing to listen to their patients and do not automatically discount 'alternative' remedies.

For instance, a lady in Evesham suffers with a congenital kidney condition and has to have regular three-monthly blood tests. Two months after starting to take royal jelly capsules she had her usual test then went to see her GP to talk about the results.

> I was told my latest blood test showed a marked improve-ment (coincidence? I don't think so). My GP was quite im-pressed by my improvement. I had told him I was taking royal jelly. He is a young GP and didn't laugh but seemed very interested. He said *perhaps* there could be something in royal jelly.

Of course, there are many instances of healthcare professionals who are either firmly convinced of the benefits of royal jelly or are at least prepared to put the substance to the test. There is the mid-wife, of whom I wrote in Chapter Seven, who recommends royal jelly to her expectant mums both as an ante-natal treatment and for boosting their energy and stamina after childbirth. Then there are the trials carried out by an SRN and monitored by a doctor with elderly patients in Loughborough. In general, it seems that there are two categories of medical professional who are happy to admit the virtues of royal jelly: those who have tried it themselves and those who have come into close contact with one or more patients who have benefited from its use.

Certainly, there seems to be no subsititue for personal recom-mendation or a practical demonstration of royal jelly's powers when it comes to spreading the news about its benefits. How often

I hear of one person in a family hearing of the substance from a friend who uses it. Nine times out of ten the whole family is taking royal jelly before the year is out.

Some people have decidedly generous ways of introducing their family and friends to the royal jelly habit. One of my correspondents, a Mr D., gave capsules to his relations as Christmas presents in 1986. The following year the recipients were his friends. He wrote to me,

> Out of the six people I gave the capsules to, three of them are now taking them regularly; my best mate is still somewhat sceptical, but he's going to buy 30 and keep it up for another month; and the other two — well, I'm still working on them!

If this 'take-up' rate on royal jelly were replicated across the country, we might no longer have such problems in financing the National Health Service, because almost 50 per cent of the population would be bubbling over with health and vitality!

I am particularly pleased whenever I hear of hard-bitten sceptics finding positive results from taking royal jelly. I know of friends who can get 'merry' on orange juice if the people around them are genuinely intoxicated through drinking alcohol. I think we all know from personal experience how easy it is to control our moods, and even our bodies, by our thoughts. This is the principle on which bio-feedback works: if you sit someone down with an instrument which bleeps in time with his pulse, he or she will be able to slow their pulse rate simply by concentrating. Then again, some of my friends swear that they lose weight simply by 'thinking thin'.

On my trip to China, I was accompanied by Sarah Bounds, Editor of the well known magazine *Here's Health*, who had never taken royal jelly. In her job she is bombarded by samples of new products and has had to develop a certain cynicism about the many benefits which they purport to bring to the consumer. However, she was soon convinced of the value of royal jelly when she began to take it on her return to Britain, and has, as happens with many sceptics, become one of the most fervent royal jelly evangelists. She wrote to me,

> I have managed to convert my father, and am about to administer a course of the capsules for animals to an aunt's sick cat! I have explained the product's origin and workings to so many people since our trip that I feel like a walking expert!

So, when someone who has totally negative feelings and expectations about royal jelly derives benefit from it, or when someone takes royal jelly to treat a particular condition and discovers very common and beneficial side-effects, I feel that their reports deserve special attention. An SRN wrote recently,

> I started both myself and my son on royal jelly capsules about four months ago as we both seemed to be very tired and listless. I am happy to say we both have regained some of our zest, and as a side bonus my son's acne is clearing up and I'm convinced my hair is less grey than it was. Or do you think this is just wishful thinking?

It could well have been that there was a psychological element in the mother's and son's increased energy levels, although this is probably *the* most commonly reported benefit. However, the improvement in the son's acne and the reversion of his mother's hair colour are less likely to have been due to auto-suggestion. Indeed, there are perfectly good scientific reasons for both 'bonuses'. The change in hair colour is not reported very freqently, but I have heard of several cases; as I explained in Chapter Three, royal jelly is the richest known source of pantothenic acid, and a lack of this vitamin can produce prematurely greying hair. It therefore follows, perhaps, that once the pantothenic acid deficiency has been made good, a smaller proportion of new hair growth will be grey.

Returning to the attitude of the medical profession to royal jelly, one of the main problems in convincing conventional doctors of the worth of this substance is that no one can prove exactly how it works. How, I am asked, can any one substance boost energy levels, cure arthritis, alleviate pain, lift depression, reverse the greying process in hair, calm hyperactive children, help both anorexia and obesity, counter both hypertension and hypotension, cure skin disorders, increase resistance to infection, lower cholesterol levels, have a beneficial effect on uro-genital dysfunction, increase mental alertness and concentration, raise red blood corpuscle counts, ease stress, increase the metabolic rate, speed up healing, help infertile couples and oxygenate the blood? Yes, it is asking a great deal of even the most sympathetic doctor to accept that royal jelly seems to have done all those things — and more.

I could point out to the profession that scientists and physicians in other countries, particularly in the Eastern bloc and Asia, have published papers reporting many of these effects, plus some others. For example, royal jelly has been used to treat malnutrition (Fatyeva, 1962), restore injured muscles (Hoja and Vittek, 1963), raise the total blood protein and improve the red blood cell count in cases of severe haemorrhaging (Tsveer, 1963). It has been shown to lower blood pressure (Beslekoev, 1964), increase the number of erythrocytes (non nucleated red blood cells) and the amount of haemoglobin, while maintaining the number of leukocytes (white blood corpuscles), lowering the cholesterol level and having a favourable effect on patients suffering from chronic coronary insufficiency (Lupachec, 1964). The Soviet scientist Mischchenko reported in 1964 that royal jelly raises blood pressure in hypotension and lowers it in hypertension, and that it normalizes blood sugar in mild diabetes and decreases vascular disturbances in artherosclerosis and angiospasms. Royal jelly has also exhibited a protective affect in laboratory animals exposed to radiation (Arbuzov et al, 1966), and has been used to treat bronchial asthma and angina pectoris (Kogut and Bogacheva, 1966), while Uzbekova stated in 1968 that it considerably increased oxygen consumption and oxidative phosphorylation in the brain.

If the medical fraternity in the West is not prepared to give sufficient weight to results produced in the East, then I could quote Barton-Wright's research carried out in England in the 1960s on arthritic patients, about which I wrote in Chapter Seven, or the work carried out in 1966 with 42 premature babies in the Department of Paediatrics in the University of Florence, which showed that royal jelly is an excellent treatment for malnutrition.

Then again, I could point to the similarity of results produced by royal jelly in humans and animals, but I cannot say for certain *how* it works, and that is the sticking point. Understandably, doctors are not like theoretical scientists who can change theories as often as they change their clothes. Everything in medicine must be proven, every 't' crossed, every 'i' dotted. Any new synthetic medicine has to go through exhaustive trials before it can be allowed on the market, and I cannot quarrel with that, given, for example, the tragic consequences which ensued from the use of thalidomide.

The difficulty is that we are not talking about a synthetic product; one which is built up from a carefully measured selection of equally synthetic ingredients — a milligramme of this, half a milligramme of that. The process is reversed: we are trying to break down a natural substance into its component parts to discover exactly what is in it, and so far that task has eluded the best analysis. An added difficulty is that, because royal jelly *is* wholly natural, its make up can vary slightly from one bee colony to another and from one season to another within the same colony. Consequently, as I explained in Chapter Two, no one can say, 'This is the definitive analysis of royal jelly'.

Such is the problem faced by scientists who have tried to synthesize royal jelly. Several have succeeded...almost. When they have tried to produce queens using the synthetic product, they may have produced a few true queens from the larval stage, but the remainder of each batch has either died, or emerged as worker bees and as bees which lie somewhere between workers and queens.

But on the other hand, natural remedies *are* often recommended by doctors — a high-fibre diet for constipation, hot honey and lemon for a cold, etc. If we go far back in history, there was a time when scurvy (vitamin C deficiency) plagued seamen. Then, in 1747, James Lind, a surgeon's mate on H.M.S. *Salisbury*, carried out an experiment to try to find an effective cure. He took a dozen sailors, all suffering from scurvy to a similar extent, and divided them into six pairs. The first pair was given cider, the second dilute sulphuric acid, the third vinegar, the fourth sea water, the fifth a herbal preparation and the sixth citrus fruit. Of course, the sixth pair were up and about in no time and were put to work looking after the others. At that time, no one knew about vitamins, and it took almost fifty years before the British Admiralty decided to issue each sailor with a daily ration of lemon juice. This decision eradicated scurvy at a stroke, but many men suffered during those fifty years of deliberation. I think you will realize the moral of this story. Doctors recommend the natural remedies for constipation and cold symptoms because they know how they work. The Admiralty prevaricated for half a century because, although they could *see* that citrus fruits were a prevention against scurvy, they did not know *how* they worked.

So, this brings me back to the burning issue — how *does* royal jelly work? I have my own theories, but there are plenty of others which have been put forward by those with more knowledge of physiology than myself.

A French physician stated that royal jelly stimulates the glandular system. As this is such a complex area of physiology, it can involve practically every other function and might explain the widespread effects reported by users. There is also a school of thought which classifies royal jelly as an 'adaptogen'; in the same family as traditional remedies like ginseng and deerhorn which have been used for centuries to revitalize the body. Yet another theory is that the discovery of hormones — testosterone and insulin-like peptides — in royal jelly might play a part. The scientists to whom I spoke in China claimed to have found as many as six hormones in royal jelly.

I am sure that, as more Western scientists carry out research into royal jelly, further discoveries will be made which will lead us closer to solving this intriguing problem. We may even identify the ingredients in the elusive 4 or 5 per cent of royal jelly which has so far defied analysis.

Suffice it to say, for now, that many thousands of people in the West, and probably millions in the East, attribute their well-being or recovery from illness to a milky-white substance produced by worker bees. To my mind, if a type of mould (penicillin) can prove to be the most successful antibiotic known to man, then it should not be too difficult to entertain the possibility that a natural foodstuff can also be a natural medicine chest.

I should dearly love to have access to a time machine and to come back to England a hundred years from now. Will our great-great-grandchildren be eating royal jelly sweets? If the National Health Service still exists, will royal jelly be available on prescription? Could there even be royal jelly wine bars on each corner where stressed executives meet after work to relax? Perhaps the world will have discovered another natural substance which is even more powerful? Whatever the future holds in store, I feel that we owe it to ourselves to make the best of Nature's store cupboard now; and as far as I am concerned, that means eating a wholesome diet, enjoying the fresh air of the countryside whenever possible, and making sure that I have my daily quota of royal jelly.

Bibliography

Barton-Wright, E.C. and Elliott, W.A., 'The pantothenic acid metabolism of rheumatoid arthritis', *The Lancet*, (October 26, 1963).

Carli, H.O. de et al, *Experimental Atherosclerosis*, (Ministerio de Asuntos Agrarios, Argentina, 1975).

Cho, Y.T. 'Studies on Royal Jelly and abnormal cholesterol and triglycerides', *American Bee Journal*, (1977).

Davis, Adelle, *Let's Stay Healthy*, (George Allen & Unwin, 1982).

Gojmerac, Walter L., *Bees, Beekeeping, Honey and Pollination*, (AVI Publishing Company Inc, Connecticut, 1980).

Hall, Dorothy, *The Natural Health Book*, (Angus & Robertson, 1979).

Kramer, K.J. et al, 'Purification of insulin-like peptides from insect haemolymph and Royal Jelly', *Insect Biochemistry*, (USA, 1982).

Krol, A. and Bornus, L., 'Amino acids in Royal jelly produced by four honeybee races', *Pszczelmicze Zeszyty Naukowe*, (Poland, 1982).

Lercker, G. et al, 'Composition of the lipid fraction of Royal Jelly and worker jelly in relation to the age of larvae', *Apidologie*, (Italy, 1984).

Mindell, Earl, *The Vitamin Bible*, (Arlington Books, 1979).

Nakajin, S. et al, 'Effect of Royal Jelly on experimental hypercholesterolemia in rabbits', *Shoyakugaku Zasshi*, Japan, 1982.

Nommenson, Etta, *Honey in the Hive*, (Winchester Press, Oklahoma, 1980).

Sanford, M.T., 'A geography of apiculture in Yucatan, Mexico', (M.A. thesis, University of Georgia, USA, 1973).

Shyu, S.T., 'The economics of the beekeeping industry in Taiwan', *Journal of Agricultural Economics*, Taiwan, 1983.

Takenaka, T. and Echigo, T., 'Proteins and peptides in Royal Jelly', *Nippon Nogeikagaku Kaishi*, Japan, 1983.

Vernon, Frank, *Beekeeping*, (Hodder and Stoughton, 1976).

Vittek, J. and Slomiany, B.L., 'Testosterone in Royal Jelly', *Experientia 40*, Basle, 1984.

Weiss, K., 'Deposition of Royal Jelly and development of queen larvae during consecutive experiments in queenless colonies of Apis mellifera', *Apidologie*, Erlangen, 1986.

Wilkinson, Steve, *M.E. and You*, (Thorsons, 1988).

Yoshida, T., and Matsuka, M. 'Trade and consumption of Royal Jelly in Japan', *Honeybee Science*, Japan, 1983.

Index

'Cassie,' Crufts Champion.

Regina Royale

Her Royal Highness The Duchess of York and Princess Beatrice.

Her Royal Highness The Princess of Wales and her two children Prince William and Prince Harry.

The author's mother — Sophie Baigler (aged 79).
Opposite: Cliff Richard
Irene Stein and her two daughters, Lisa and Jane.
(Photo: Steven Hampshire)

Top: A queen bee emerging from the cell.

Middle: A queen cell with royal jelly.

Right: A research worker at Fragrance Mountain placing larvae in cells.

Mrs Thatcher, the British Prime Minister, being presented with a range of royal jelly products by the author.

Analysis of royal jelly products using Kirlian photography techniques.

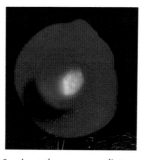

1. See how the energy radiates out. This is called, in Kirlian terms, 'the globule effect'. The mass of red colour indicates energy which is in a readily available form.

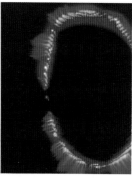

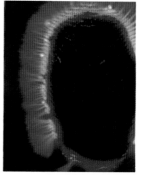

2. A fingertip before applying royal jelly and Vitamin E — the normal human aura.

3. A fingertip after applying the cream — note the extra energy given off. This is indicated by the greater regularity and intensity of the white lines.

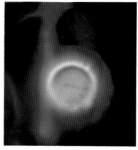

4. Energy radiated by a freeze-dried capsule, and a capsule which purports to contain fresh royal jelly and vegetable oil.

5. Energy shown to radiate from a fresh royal jelly capsule.